100 Proven and Surefire Ways to Meet, Date, Attract, and Seduce Women: Guaranteed and Tested Results for Scoring with Women

by Don Diebel

GEMINI PUBLISHING COMPANY
818 Lois Street, Suite A
Kerrville, TX 78028

I0162464

Email: getgirls@getgirls.com

Web Site: https://www.getgirls.com

ISBN: 9780937164488

Table of Contents:

Introduction

Since my early twenties, I set out on a lifelong journey to find out what it takes to meet, attract, seduce, and succeed with women. What works and what doesn't work.

Through lots of dating experience, research, and a lot of trial and error in dating and seduction techniques I began to notice very consistent and predictable patterns of success with women. I came up with 100 proven and surefire ways to help you score with women, which is the basis of this book.

We were all put on this earth for a purpose and we all possess God-given talents. My mission and purpose on earth is to help men like yourself succeed with women beyond your wildest dreams and fill your life with lots of love, romance, fun, and intimacy.

I believe that a fulfilling relationship with a woman is the most wonderful gift this life has to offer on earth. And that is the purpose of this book – To help you get all the love and romance you deserve with women.

If you will follow and practice my proven 100 ways to meet, date, attract, and seduce women, your love life will skyrocket. You will also gain a distinct advantage over your competition. You will enjoy levels of success with women you may never have imagined possible. I guarantee it!

As you read my 100 proven ways to meet, date, attract, and seduce women, reflect on how you treat women, your behavior around women, how you act on dates, how you approach women, how you talk to women, how you romance women, your grooming habits and how you dress around women, etc.

I'm sure you will discover some mistakes you have been making with women. And I hope my book will serve as a wake-up call on why you're not succeeding with women like you should and you will take measures to correct your mistakes so you can start succeeding with women instead of being a failure and spending all those lonely nights alone.

In closing, I wish you much success and happiness with women. Remember, just one of my 100 ways to meet, date, attract, and seduce women can dramatically change the direction of your dating and love life for the better.

Dating Tips and Advice

1. Succeed with Women by Thinking Positive

Think positive

Why do some men succeed with women while others fail time and time again? You should know the answer by now. What's the major difference between the man with all the beautiful girls and the guy with none? What's the difference? The way the man thinks! That's the difference.

Start Thinking Right and You'll Succeed with Women Beyond Your Wildest Dreams

The man who is successful with women thinks in terms of 100% success at all times. While the guy who fails with women thinks in terms of failure most of the time. Perhaps, in your case, you've been having a hard time meeting, dating or seducing girls (or all three) because you subconsciously expect to have a hard time! When you try to meet a girl, you fail. Why? Because you subconsciously expect to fail. When you ask a girl for a date, you get turned down. Why? Because you subconsciously expect to get turned down. And it's the same story all the way into the bedroom.

Women easily sense this lack of confidence in you and react accordingly. Actually, you are beaten before you even start! So, guys, it's time to change your attitude. Think positive and expect to succeed with every woman you meet or approach. It will make a world of difference in your love life.

2. Shy Dating - A Few Things To Know

If you find yourself shy dating people, then there are a few things you should know that will allow you to come out of your comfort zone. It is advised to try them all at the same time so that there is a greater chance of you having a wonderful dating experience.

Some things you can do are to look for people with similar interests as you, be comfortable, be prepared, don't expect your date to be perfect, and talk about her, not always about yourself.

One of the easiest ways to overcome your shyness is to find some people with similar interests as you. The main reason for this is so you can have something to talk about naturally. Take Role Playing Card Games for example. If you are a fan of the game Magic, or Dungeons and Dragons, then finding a social group that plays this

4

is beneficial for you because you will be able to instantly talk about something you are interested in - card games!

Another way to overcome your shyness is to learn to be comfortable in your surroundings. The easiest way to do this is to get out more. Go to more social outings and just start talking to people. You will gradually begin to learn how people interact with each other.

Another great way to do this is to go to community ice breaker sessions. If you go to college or live on campus, this is also a great way to break the ice. Go to Meetup places online where they meet locally and do activities together. This is great because they have cool things you can do that are already pre planned so that you won't have to stress about planning for events. All you have to do is participate in the ice breakers and get to know people.

Also, be prepared for anything, namely meeting people with different interests and different topics of conversations. Stay well read in current news events by spending about ten minutes each day scrolling through all the top stories, or listen to the radio while going to work. That way you will be able to put some context to what the people are saying.

Don't expect your dates to be perfect. They are different than you are. Get your partner to talk about themselves and resist saying "I", "Me", or "My" statements. Ask questions about them and then follow up with some things you have read or have done that are related to that. These are just a few ways you can overcome your shy dating habits and have some awesome dates.

3. How You Can Start Dating Beautiful Women

Let's face it, men like dating beautiful women. I don't think anyone would dispute the notion that most men are attracted to healthy, fit, and beautiful women. Having a stunningly gorgeous woman on his arm is a huge boost to the male ego, particularly when a man's friends and acquaintances have an obviously positive reaction to his date. So how can a guy, even an average guy, have more success in dating very attractive women?

Dave is what you'd probably consider just an average guy. He's not extraordinarily good looking, and he certainly isn't rich. But Dave is the envy of his friends because in recent years he's managed to date a series of extremely attractive women. Dave says he's learned a lot about dating beautiful women and he's the better man for it. "I used to think that I didn't have a chance with a really hot female," Dave recounted. "I used to be afraid to approach them at all. I just knew that I was going to get shot down in flames. I was paralyzed, really... paralyzed with fear."

So how did Dave overcome his nerves and begin to find more attractive women to date? He says there's a lot of things the average guy has to overcome to hook up with the most gorgeous girls, but the biggest one is the fear of failure. Dave says men have to let that fear go before they have any chance to land the most beautiful women to date. The key to dating beautiful women is to first change the way you look at yourself.

"I had to allow myself to fail," Dave said. "One day I saw this guy I knew from work out on a date with an absolutely drop-dead gorgeous woman. He made less money than me, and he certainly wasn't any better looking. But when I saw those two together, I realized that there was something about his approach that was different from mine. I decided that it must be that he wasn't afraid to take a chance despite the fact that he might get turned down".

Dave says that it was then that he resolved to change his approach. Instead of worrying about being turned down by a gorgeous woman, he decided that he would accept each failure as one step closer to success. When dating beautiful women, our Dave decided that it was simply a numbers game. The more women he asked out, the more chances he had of getting a "yes".

"My new outlook changed my life," Dave explained. "I decided that I wasn't going to be afraid. I convinced myself that if I had to ask five hot girls for a date before I would get one, then I could better accept getting turned down. If I saw a gorgeous girl and asked her out and got a no, then that meant I only needed three more no's before I'd get that yes. And now, here I am, dating beautiful women and enjoying my life like never before".

4. Age Differences in Dating

Some people are attracted to members of the opposite sex that have a significant age difference from them. They may prefer dating someone that is younger or older. This is often a matter of personal preference and there are many reasons that people choose these relationships. It is dependent on the individual person and their life.

Some people are attracted to members of the opposite sex that have a significant age difference from them. They may prefer dating someone that is younger or older. This is often a matter of personal preference and there are many reasons that people choose these relationships. It is dependent on the individual person and their life.

In most cases, women are attracted to older men. This may be due to the fact that women mature at a younger age than men. In order for women to date a guy that is as mature as they are, they have to resort to older men. For some women, younger men that are less mature are not an issue. They enjoy having a relationship with them and it all works out fine for both people. However, for some women having a mate that is less mature is almost like having a child. They do not want to have to mother their partner. They want the compatibility and the even keel. Again, this is all a matter of personal preference.

Men also have attractions and relationships with females that are a different age than them. Again, the reasons are just as diversified. They may seek an older or younger woman depending on their preference. They may also look for someone that is around the same age.

Some men that are less mature like to find a woman that is closer to their maturity level. In this situation, they would most often date a woman that is younger than them. This would help them to feel that they are fulfilling their role as the man of the relationship. It is hard to present yourself as a strong man and as being capable of caring for your mate in a relationship, if you are not mature enough to fulfill this role. However, there are also some men that seek older women to have a relationship with. They want the mothering type of relationship and they want to be able to act a little less mature and be taken care of themselves.

For some people age has no influence on them at all. They date people based on their attraction or traits that they are looking for.

They are compatible with a person and want to spend time with them. There are times that they will not even know how old the person that they are talking with is for a while. They are not worried about age. There is no factoring of age to consider.

These people are sometimes the happiest and in some cases have the best relationships. This is due to the fact that they are not into trivial things and they are really looking for personality and internal traits. They are not worried about looks, age, or other trivial factors.

Every person is different. You may have to date people of different ages to determine what is best for you. If you are new to the dating scene, it is especially important to determine what works best for you. This is important to determine before you try to get involved in a serious relationship. If not, you are setting yourself up for failure and misery.

5. Are You In A Love Depression

Are you in a love depression? This is where your heart has been broken and you feel low about it. You may believe that you will never have another romance. Here's what to do if you are in a love depression.

First of all, you need to recognize that, however painful, this is a temporary period in your life. You will get through your love depression. But, you may need help.

Turn to your friends and family during this tough period in your life. They will always be there for you. Don't be afraid to cry on their shoulders. One of the ways you will know when you have come out of the love depression is when you yourself are bored with talking about your ex.

But, if your friends and family get tired of hearing about your ex before you are healed, it may behoove you to go into counseling. A trained therapist can help you work through the break up issues. By talking to a counselor, you will be able to identify many issues in your life. Some of these will be about why you and your ex broke up. Others will help you be a better boyfriend or girlfriend in the future.

Sometimes talk therapy isn't enough. When this happens, you need to see a psychiatrist who can put you on antidepressant medication. Prozac, Paxil, and other SSRIs can make a big difference in how you feel about the world. Don't be embarrassed to ask for medical help when you need it.

There are other things you can do for yourself when you are in a love depression. For instance, when you go to the gym to work out, you not only improve your body, you also improve your mood. Getting your body moving sends chemicals to the brain which elevate your mood.

Pampering yourself can also help you believe that you are a worthwhile person. Getting a massage can bring physical relief to your weary body.

Sometimes eating, in moderation, can soothe your soul. Chocolate, ice cream, and comfort foods all help ease the pain of a break up. Don't overdo it and gain too much weight though, because you don't want to ruin your physique.

Perhaps the best tonic for love depression though, is falling in love with someone new. Remember that in order to do that, you have to get back in the game. Don't believe that you have to be 100 percent ready for a new relationship before you start dating again. When someone asks you out or strikes your fancy, have coffee with them. Go to the ballgame with a friend who might be interested in being more.

At some point, you have to get back on the dating scene. Whether talking to your friends, going into therapy, getting some psychiatric medication, or treating your condition yourself, you need to work out a way to cure your love depression. The sooner you do, the sooner you'll feel a lot better.

6. Do Not Smother Women

The "Smothering Technique" that turns women off:

This is how I describe this technique: After first meeting a girl, you call her all the time, sometimes twice or more a day at her work and at home. And when you can't reach her, you get all upset.

You keep thinking to yourself, where in the hell is she? Is she seeing someone else, is she trying to avoid me, has she lost interest in me, etc. You just keep worrying and worrying. When you do get in touch with her you ask her, "Where have you been, I've been trying to get in touch with you!"

And you keep repeating this pattern of calling her all the time to where it reaches the point where you become a pest. She is totally turned off and needs her space and all you are doing is driving her further away from you.

Please, guys don't do this! It's only going to backfire when you try to smother her. How often should you call? Just calling her every other day will be just fine and don't linger on the phone for hours as if you had nothing better to do with your life and your whole world revolves around her. Just keep it brief and say what you have to say. By not calling so often this will make her think about you. She will be wondering what you're doing and she might even wonder why you haven't called and that's good because it gets her to think about you.

7. Effective Dating Advice for Men

The "classic", or generic date, not to be confused with the unconventional creative / inventive date, consists of entertainment, followed by a meal, then a walk under the stars, and finally the leave taking. The entertainment usually defaults to a movie, though a live performance, a play or a concert, makes for a richer experience. There is no need to spend "big bucks" in an expensive restaurant. A simple meal in an "atmospheric" neighborhood cafe, the scarred wooden table covered by a stained, checkered cloth, with a guttering candle in an old wine bottle between the two of you as you scoop up forkfuls of pungently spiced, chewy spaghetti, occasionally catching shy glimpses of each other's eyes... all this will do just fine. Then the walk home, the time for quiet reflection and expressing feelings by glances and occasional words, this tops off a satisfying evening.

As you walk with her, by her side, matching your step to hers, in cadence, in harmony, she has the opportunity to take your hand... if she is so moved. Holding hands comes naturally, if it comes at all. Do not force unwanted attention on her! "Making a move on her" is neither required of you, nor desirable. She will touch you if she has been touched by your presence. If she wants to be touched, she will touch you.

Time for parting. "Goodbye. I enjoyed the evening and the pleasure of your company." You may take her hand, if she is amenable, for a goodbye hand squeeze. If she offers her cheek, you may kiss it, likewise her lips... if she offers. Respond, rather than initiate. Physical closeness is her gift to you, given if and when the time is right, and a first date is rather soon. "It was a wonderful evening. May I see you again?" It is the end of an evening... and a beginning.

8. Loneliness

There is a fundamental human need for companionship, for a sympathetic ear, for reassurance, for hearing our feelings and sentiments echoed back, for touching and being touched. Being alone is sensory deprivation, slow torture, and our souls cry out for the company of a kindred spirit, for the comfort that only a friend can give, for someone who can fill the emptiness, who can share the isolated moments of our existence. Loneliness weakens the spirit. It consumes our strength and dims our inner flame. It tempts us to wallow in self-pity, to descend into a kind of gloomy rapture, depressed and paralyzed, yet at the same time glorying in our misery, suffering proudly in our own private hell. For all that, loneliness is a state of mind, a sickness of the soul rather than an external condition, and it is entirely within our power to fight it, and perhaps work toward healing it.

Resisting loneliness is more than simply a matter of "keeping busy", of immersing yourself in so many activities that you have no time to reflect on your sad state. It involves following your interests, improving your skills, developing yourself as a multifaceted individual. It means going out and meeting people, making contacts, learning to survive in a social context. It means living your dream, not at some future time when you might finally be in a relationship, but NOW.

Aloneness is the riddle we must solve in order to be worthy of the companionship of others, and therein lies the central paradox of being alone - that it can either ennoble, or degrade. The essential difference between aloneness and loneliness is the anguish, the acute hunger for contact that the lonely suffer. Could we consider solitude a necessary journey of discovery, a crisis that may ultimately purify and strengthen us, then we would emerge from this Dark Night of the Soul uplifted and exalted, more fully realized as a person. Once comfortable in our own company, reconciled to the austere beauty of silence, of privacy, of total self-sufficiency, only then can we travel onward and explore the horizons of interaction, of exchange, or binding with our fellow humans.

9. Overcoming Nervousness with Women

Meeting a woman for the first time (or even the fifth time) can precipitate a crisis of nerves. It is an all too familiar feeling, the knot in the stomach, the tightening behind the jaw, the sweating, turning red, stammering, and being at a total loss for words. You panic, freeze up, and it is a major relief escaping from the situation. Another opportunity blown.

Beneath nervousness lurks shattering fear, the stuff of childhood nightmares. Admit the fear. Confront it. You fear making a fool of yourself. You fear messing things up. You fear rejection. You fear ridicule. You fear mocking laughter. You fear what fear itself is doing to you, breaking down your resolve and triggering the reflex to run and hide. Yet, you can grit your teeth and fight back. Know you can be afraid, and still do what needs to be done.

"I must not fear. Fear is the mind-killer. Fear is the little-death that brings total obliteration. I will face my fear. I will permit it to pass over me and through me. And when it has gone past I will turn the inner eye to see its path. Where the fear has gone there will be nothing. Only I will remain."

"Bene Gesserit Litany Against Fear" from Frank Herbert's "DUNE"

Learn to control the physiological manifestations of nervousness. Breathing is the key. In the midst of an attack of nerves, you are taking frequent shallow breaths, hyperventilating, superoxygenating your blood, overloading your system with adrenaline. Discipline your breathing. Inhale deeply, but only at the rate of once per six seconds. Hold breath, count cadence, 1---2---3---4---5---6, breathe, hold, 1---2, exhale. The rhythm becomes automatic, no longer requiring your conscious attention. Now, silently, within yourself, chant a favorite poem, or an appropriate mantra, "I-shall-endure, I-shall-endure...". Your pulse rate slows, the tension drains from you, and the perspiration dries as calm returns.

Wall yourself off from the woman across from you. Need, desperation, and loneliness have plunged you into a state of hyper acute emotional sensitivity. It is as though your feelings were an open wound, and a single touch means agony. Weakness! Vulnerability! Visualize a shield, construct an invisible barrier in your mind between the two of you. You are, as yet, strangers to each other, all possibilities unrealized, and you cannot, will not impinge upon each other, neither physically nor yet in the realm of feelings. You are only just "establishing diplomatic relations". It is a small, safe beginning.

In time, you will learn to harness the motive force, the raw power that your mind and body's reaction to challenge provides. Fear can mobilize, rather than paralyze. Think of it as a resource, a reservoir of energy. Harness it. Use it.

10. A Man's Guide to Re-Entering the Singles Scene

If you are just getting out of a committed relationship you may need a few tips for re-entering the singles scene. While the singles scene may not have changed tremendously during your relationship, you probably have. Being in a committed relationship is much different from being involved in the singles scene and you may need a few tips before re-entering the dating world. You'll need to relearn previously mastered skills that may have been forgotten such as making yourself appear attractive, asking out someone and planning a date and reading the signals of other singles. Additionally, if online dating sites didn't exist when you were courting your previous partner you may need to learn a little about this before re-entering the singles scene. It may take some time to get back into the singles scenes but these tips will help to ease the transition.

The key to attracting potential partners is to make yourself appear as attractive as possible. This may not be as simple as it sounds. You may look in the mirror and see yourself as attractive physically, mentally and emotionally but your opinion is not what is most important in the dating scene. What you believe is attractive may not be perceived that way by other singles so it is important to have a good understanding about what your potential partners may identify as attractive. Try using your previous relationship as a guideline for making yourself appear as attractive as possible. Think back to what it was about you that attracted your previous partner and try to emphasize that feature or characteristic. For example if your previous partner frequently complimented you on your broad shoulders and your thoughtfulness, you may want to wear clothes that accentuate your shoulders and take care to treat new acquaintances thoughtfully. Understanding what potential partners may find attractive and emphasizing these features are essential to a man who is ready to re-enter the singles scene.

If you were in your previous relationship for a long time, it has probably been quite a while since you have had to ask someone out. The key to success in the singles scene is the ability to ask others out on dates and have them agree to go on a date with you. This is not a difficult skill but it is one that a man may need to brush up on if he has been out of the singles scene for awhile. If you want to have a great deal of success in asking people out, be confident without appearing arrogant. This will make you seem like you are sure of yourself but not self-centered and will make you more desirable. Also, when asking someone out, offer specific suggestions for what you would like to do on the date. Just asking someone if they would be interested in getting together sometime is not nearly as effective as asking if they would be interested in joining you for dinner and dancing on a certain date. One of the most important aspects of the singles scene is the ability to ask people out successfully and many men may need a few tips on this as they prepare to re-enter the singles scene.

In the singles scene, it is also very important to be able to read the signals that others are giving off. This skill will help determine if others are interested in you but this ability may have become rusty while you were in a committed relationship because you became used to your partner and the subtle ways they communicated with you without using words. In the singles scene however, singles are constantly giving off subtle signals that let you know whether or not you should approach them. Understanding body language that indicates that the other person is not interested will help you avoid wasting your time on someone who isn't interested in you. A person who crosses their arms or turns away from you and averts eye contact is likely not interested in pursuing a relationship with you. Conversely, someone who smiles at you from afar, makes eye contact and angles their body towards you is probably interested in getting to know you better and may be open to going on a first date with you.

Online dating and web sites that host personal ads are becoming increasingly popular. If these weren't available when you were courting your previous partner or you are unaware of how these sites work, you may want to explore the Internet as an opportunity to meet new potential partners. Understanding how online dating sites work will help you to navigate your way around this cyber singles scene. While you may meet the love of your life online, it is important to exercise restraint in dating someone you meet online as it is very easy to deceive others online.

Re-entering the dating scene after a long relationship can be tricky but hopefully these tips will help to guide you through the singles scene. It's important to remember that the dating scene probably hasn't changed much since you were involved in it. Most likely, you have changed more than the dating scene so it just may take a little time before you remember how to successfully navigate the singles scene. Also, keep in mind that being yourself and having fun is the most effective way to meet people.

How to Talk to Women

11. Conversation Sins with Women

Here are a couple of deadly conversation sins that will cause you to strike out with women. You must never commit these deadly sins:

SIN #1 - Bragging about yourself and your accomplishments. There's no faster way of driving single women away from you than by constantly talking about yourself and your own great accomplishments. Forget about yourself. The whole art of conversation with a woman is to become interested in her rather than trying to get her interested in you. Remember that most people are interested in themselves morning, noon, and night. Never forget this fact. After all, why should a woman be interested in you unless you are interested in her first? Just put your ego aside and concentrate solely on her and her interests.

SIN #2 - Talking too vulgarly and crudely. In the beginning, when you meet a woman and you start talking sexually and making vulgar remarks, you are going to turn her off and you will get nowhere with her. Don't tell her things like, "You sure have a great set of tits" or "I'd love to make love to you." This is showing her lack of respect and she won't appreciate it. They want to be treated like a lady and not some whore. Another mistake is propositioning her for sex in a crude manner with statements like, "Let's go f--k," or "I sure would like to f--k you." Treat her like a lady and don't act like a horny dog with uncontrollable hormones. You'll make a much better impression on her by keeping cool and calm and non-sexual and non-threatening. You will stand out favorably from the other guys she's used to being around that act like animals.

12. **Please do not Make These Conversation Mistakes**

SIN #1 - Interrupting her during conversation. This is a quick way of becoming unpopular with her and even being disliked. Interrupting her when she's trying to say something is an insult and can hurt her feelings. If you are doing this, it stems from your ego problem of wanting to feel important, to be heard, and to be recognized.

Don't commit this deadly sin and just put your ego aside and concentrate completely on what she is saying. Focus all of your undivided attention on her and don't butt in. Hear her out. If you listen closely enough, you might even learn something of value.

SIN #2 - Not listening to her. Nobody likes to be ignored. Failure to pay attention to her while she is talking is an insult. It is a form of rejection and nobody likes to feel rejected. Don't be preoccupied with what's going on around you and tune her out. Don't focus on other women while she's talking to you either.

If she's talking about a subject you have no interest in, don't spend your time trying to come up with ways to change the topic of conversation to something that you enjoy talking about. Hear her out!

Don't make this mistake either. Let's say she's talking about a subject you're really interested in and you get so anxious to put your two cents worth in and comments, you spend your time going over in your mind what you are going to say rather than listening attentively to her.

13. Keeping a Relationship Going

It has always amazed me how so many potential relationships just fizzle out. They start out great, but once the initial romance and infatuation phase wears off then you begin to lose interest in each other. Why?

Well, sometimes it's because one or both parties don't put forth the effort to keep the relationship alive. It takes a lot of work to find and start a relationship, but it also takes a lot of work to sustain one.

The point I'm trying to make is that you shouldn't give up on a relationship after the glamor has worn off. Don't wrongly assume that you have no future with her because the relationship is not as exciting as it was in the beginning.

You must do your part to nurture the relationship and keep the fires burning. Don't take her for granted just because you've been dating for a few weeks. You must make a continuous effort to romance her and keep her attracted to you. Show and tell how much you care for her.

In closing, I would like to give you some more advice. Give a relationship time to develop. I have made a lot of mistakes in the past by dumping women after just a few dates. I didn't take the time to get to know them and find out what they were like on the inside where it counts. At the time my brain was between my legs and all I was interested in was using women just for sex, then moving on to my next conquest (victim). This I'm not proud of to admit. I'm much older now and much wiser and interested in what women are like on the inside.

14. **Understand What is Good to Say and What is Not**

When you are dating singles online, you need to learn about how to talk to them. One major issue is using abbreviations. People have been shown to have a poor response to messages that exchange u for you, or ur for your or you're. Any shortening of words like this isn't attractive, and neither is leaving out capitalization or punctuation such as apostrophes.

Think about it, when you are communicating with someone online, they have very little to go on when it comes to figuring out who you are. Your picture and profile give them some idea, but it is your words and how you use them that really show your colors to other people.

Also, when you are dating singles online, don't use terms that sound like pick-up lines. Guys in particular should avoid referring to a woman as beautiful or sexy. While the guy might think this is a compliment, if used too early a woman might think the guy is only after one thing, and this usually turns women off. Be Honest!

There are few pieces of advice more important than this. Trying to be someone you aren't can take many forms, such as having an old picture up, leaving things off your profile that are a big part of who you are, or putting things on your profile that aren't true. More people complain of dishonesty in online dating than anything else.

Dating singles online can be very rewarding, and you just may find the perfect someone. By getting acquainted with the guidelines and etiquette you will impress people, and by being true to yourself you will enjoy your experience a lot more.

15. Talking About Sex

I can't think of a better way to turn women off, have her lose respect for you, and make her not want to see you again.

I know you probably think about sex most of the time and you may not see any harm in expressing your feelings about sex while on a date.

Once you get to know a girl she may feel more comfortable talking about sex, but doing this on your very first date is taboo. Here are some examples of questions and comments pertaining to sex you must never ask or discuss on a first date:

1. How are you in bed?
2. How many sex partners have you had?
3. How many one-night stands have you had?
4. Do you believe in having sex on the first date?
5. Are you horny tonight?
6. Can I spend the night with you?
7. Will you make love to me?
8. Talk about what a strong sex drive you have.
9. Talk about what a great lover you are.

Trust me guys, women don't like it when you get too sexually aggressive on a first date. Even worse is all during the date; all you can talk about is sex or things of a sexual nature. When you do this, she will get the impression that all you want to do is use women for sex and you treat women like a piece of meat.

When you focus too much on sex, it shows that you don't have much respect for her. You'll make a much better impression on her by being a complete gentleman and keep your hormones in check (being romantic is just fine, just don't get too sexual).

In closing, I can almost guarantee you that if you come on too strong sexually on your first date; you really hurt your chances for a second date.

Your best strategy is to take things slow and let nature take its

Your best strategy is to take things slow and let nature take its course. It takes time to develop a relationship and when you both develop chemistry and attraction towards each other, intimacy follows.

16. **When not to Talk**

When talking to women on your first few dates there are going to be some subjects that she will not want to discuss. These can be topics that bring back bad memories, causes her pain, things she's trying to forget about, or just plain thinks it's none of your business.

Trust me guys, when a woman says that she doesn't want to talk about a certain subject, that's exactly what she means. Just change the subject and respect her wishes.

As an example, you ask her if she has ever been married before and you start asking her questions about her marriage and she says she doesn't want to talk about it. You ignore her request and all during your date you go on and on questioning her about her previous marriage. And she continues to tell you that she doesn't want to talk about it.

At some point she is going to be pissed off at you for trying to pry information out of her on a subject she does not want to discuss. You make a fool of yourself and she does not care to see you again. It's just not worth it guys. Just shut up when she says she does not want to talk about something.

In my opinion you should avoid talking about highly sensitive and personal issues on your first few dates, especially previous relationships.

17. **Body Language to Use When Talking to Women**

You need to be aware some body language tips to help you become a better conversationalist with women:

Nod In Your Conversations - In conversations, nod while she is speaking. Slow, repeated nodding indicates general affirmation. Your nodding shows that you understand what's being said. It says, "Yes. Go on." - and invites her to continue speaking. Add to your physical vocabulary quick nodding, to show, "Ah yes, I understand!"

Avoid A Rigid Head Around Women - Avoid having a rigidly held head and stiff neck. In body language, such a stance is a conversation killer, especially if combined with a blank facial expression. By contrast, if you get into the habit of nodding, you'll encourage continued contact.

Lean Forward While Listening to Her - Lean forward slightly while she is talking to you. You'll show that you're listening and interested. She will feel complimented, and will feel encouraged to continue talking. Refrain from leaning back with your hands behind your head. That posture gives off messages of judgment, skepticism, and boredom - and will inhibit her from speaking.

18. Places to Meet Women to Date

Meeting women that you would actually want to date and, maybe eventually, bring home to meet mom and dad, isn't as hard as it sounds. There is, of course, the singles scene out in the bars and clubs all over town but I don't recommend that one. It's not that just bad girls go to bars; it's that it is hard to tell the good ones from the bad ones.

You meet women at work, too, but, there again, I don't recommend dating them. The problem with that is that, if things don't work out, you will still have to work together and the situation could be awkward to say the least.

Your friends know women that you haven't met - sisters, cousins, etc. Ask them to introduce you to them. But, big brother, do avoid blind dates. Those things hardly ever work out and you can spend a lot of money for a very uncomfortable evening.

The best places to meet women that you might actually want to date are at clubs and organizations that you belong to. You will already have something in common with them and will have had the opportunity to see them interact with other people and that tells you a lot about a person. If you aren't already involved with any clubs or organizations then, for heaven sakes, join some. Find ones that are all about something you are interested in. There are clubs and organizations that cover just about anything you can think of from astronomy to zoology and single women are involved in all of them.

Church is an excellent place to meet women. If there aren't any single women in the church you go to now, visit other churches until you find one where there are single women. The church itself will provide you with an opportunity to get to know the woman before you ask her for a date. You will be a lot more comfortable and so will she.

Get involved in civic organizations. Women love men who are civic minded. They admire men who are willing to "give back". And what about political campaigns? You will meet a lot of young women who are passionate about politics.

If all else fails, join a good online dating service. You will meet a lot of eligible women. You can read their profiles and see pictures of them. After you get to know one well enough to ask her for a face-to-face meeting, be sure that you plan the meeting during daylight hours and in a public place.

19. Rejection from Women

Rejection, rejection by a woman, rejection by the woman, the woman who has captured your thoughts, the woman whose smile sends shivers of warmth down your spine, the woman whose touch you dream of ... this icy doom fills you with dread. It is the utter desolation of helplessness. It is the worm of self-doubt. It is the gripping fear that warns you to abandon hope. Rejection is a part of everyday life. People are turned down for raises, refused promotions, declined for loans, and passed over for recognition. Rejection is not final. Rejection is not ruin. Indeed, rejection can be the precursor to eventual success.

There is nothing personal about rejection. It happens to everyone. It is part of "the cost of doing business". It is intimately connected with risk taking. Every worthwhile endeavor at some point involves the risk of failure. This is what makes life interesting.

It is only by risking our persons from one hour to another that we live at all. And often enough our faith beforehand in an uncertified result is the only thing that makes the result come true.
William James

Consider a rejection as a "second opinion" of sorts. The woman who rejects you might well have sounder judgment in the matter of a possible relationship than you. She may have compelling reasons for her conclusion that you are ill suited for each other, saving the both of you a great deal of future grief. This does not, of course, mean you are worthless as a person, just that she was not meant for you, and that you should find someone else.

There are techniques that can remove some of the sting from the fear of rejection. Simply "scoping the situation out", proceeding in small steps, rather than taking the grand plunge all at once is a prudent method of risk management. Asking a woman you have just met to become intimately involved with you is an enterprise almost certain to fail. Asking her to share five minutes over a cup of coffee is a more modest proposal, one much more likely to meet with her approval (after that, she may hint, or even let you know outright if she is willing to go farther). Tackle tricky situations in small increments.

When you do face rejection, and you will, accept it with good cheer. Bounce back and try again (presumably with a different woman). Continued life experience will desensitize you to the trauma of having doors slammed in your face. You learn to survive. You learn to go on. You learn to keep trying.

20. How to Find the Perfect Woman for You

It must be really tough. Do you think you are just a victim of bad luck and that's the reason Ms. Perfect hasn't appeared in your life yet?

Or have you decided that maybe Ms. Perfect only exists on movie screens and not out here in the real world? BINGO! You've got it. She doesn't exist anywhere except in your imagination and on movie screens.

The truth of the matter is that the reason Ms. Perfect hasn't appeared has nothing to do with your luck, good or bad, but everything to do with you and the fact that you are busy looking for a person that doesn't exist! You can't date with your eyes closed and some impossible dream in your head. You'll get so caught up in this whole exercise of dating that you forget to look for the qualities you seek! You haven't met the person of your dreams because you aren't looking for the things that will make them close enough to perfect for you.

You are so confident that every woman you have met could not give you what you wanted. But what was it that you wanted in the first place? Once you are sure of what you want, you will know exactly what to look for in your woman. What are the qualities that you feel are necessary in a person? What are the attributes you are willing to make a compromise on? Have you thought about all these?

Remember, that nobody on this earth is perfect. Everybody has faults…some are bigger faults than other faults. Some are faults you can overlook and some are faults that you couldn't overlook on your best day and if she was the most beautiful, most sexy woman on the planet.

When you meet a woman, remember, however hard you try to impress others, you cannot control their thought processes. Instead, it's far better to concentrate on your needs and desires, and how much of what you need would be fulfilled if you dated this woman.

21. How to Get Your Girlfriend Back

Rule #1 use these tactics on how to get your girlfriend back. They will work. Just make sure that no matter what you do you are honest. Now is not the time to try to pretend like you don't care or you're not hurting. Don't be a whiner, but if you love her let her know.

One of the most common things people do after they break up, is try to explain everything to their ex in the hopes that their ex will change their mind. We convince ourselves that if our ex just understood they would realize they shouldn't break up after all. Unfortunately, this is also one of the biggest mistakes most people make. If you want to know how to get your girlfriend back, the right way, read on.

The truth of the matter is that if you are constantly calling or texting your ex to explain everything, you are making yourself look pathetic and desperate...and that is not how you want your ex to think of you.

You need to give her time to really miss you and think that it may really be over. If you're calling her all the time you're telling her that she can take her time since you've made it very obvious that you want her back. She may think of you as her 'backup plan' (without even realizing it) and that may push her to go out and start dating.

If, on the other hand, you keep your distance she will be a little unsure of where the two of you stand and if she has any doubts at all about the breakup, she will give it a lot more thought. So, rule # 1 is to keep your distance at first.

Rule # 2 is to live your life. This may seem impossible when you are still in so much pain, but it's important for two reasons.

For one thing, while you may not be able to totally put her out of

your mind, you will at least have some distractions if you're hanging out with friends and family.

Another thing is that it is likely that she will hear that you're out having fun and that will remind her of the fun times the two of you used to spend together.

Rule # 3, don't hook up with anyone else. If you're ex hears that you're out fooling around with other women she might be jealous, but she's also likely to get mad and go out and hook up with someone else too. That's not really what you want, is it?

22. Tips for Dating a Woman with Kids

Dating a woman with kids poses its own challenges. In most relationships, the chemistry is between a man and a woman. When you are dating a woman with kids, the relationship becomes between a man, woman, and child.

First of all, you should know that it is harder for single moms to find dates than it is for women without children. Many men shy away from single moms because they don't want to deal with the challenges of children.

This means that a single mom may be more approachable and eager to date you.

That doesn't mean that she'll have lots of time for you though. Dating a woman with kids means that you compete for her time, and her kids will always come first. A single mom will probably be working full time, going to little league practice or ballet lessons, and having a social life besides. Where she fits you into the picture may be limited. For instance, she may want to see you for dinner on Wednesday nights only – because that's dad's night with the kids. She may only be available for dates every other Saturday. You will have to decide together when to get to know her kids. It is bad parenting to bring a succession of men into her kids' lives. So,

despite the fact that her kids are the most important thing in the world to her, you may find yourself being excluded from this realm for six months or more. When you do meet the kids, you have to decide how you will relate to them. They're not your children, but you will want them on your side. While younger children are easier to impress – just toss a ball or draw with them – older kids have their own activities.

Most children wish that their mom and dad would get back together. They are likely to see you as a threat to this fantasy. In almost all cases, there is at least initial resistance to having you in their mom's life. You will also have the challenges of authority when you are dating a woman with kids. When you give an instruction to a child, they are likely to say "you're not my dad." Think through your response to this challenge carefully ahead of time as it may set the tone for the rest of your relationship with the child.

Another problem with dating a woman with children is that it can get quite expensive. After you have settled into a relationship and you know her kids, dates often become "family" outings. Instead of going for pizza and beer with your girlfriend, you are likely to end up at Chuck E. Cheese's with the kids in tow. Forget going to an amusement park unless the kids get to come along.

And, sex becomes tricky when you are dating a woman with kids. Some women are reluctant to bring you home for an overnight stay because of the message that will be sent to the kids. She is also not likely to want to come over to your place because that involves finding someone to watch the kids.

If she does allow you into her bedroom, you may well be interrupted by children at a key moment. Be prepared for children to invade every aspect of your life. One final note – if you do get involved with a woman's children and subsequently break up with her, you will almost always lose your relationship with the kids. In this case, you will suffer from double heartbreak. This is not to say that you should avoid dating a woman with kids. Instead, be aware of the challenges – and the possibilities.

Dating Ethic Women

23. Latin Single Women – What to Know When Dating a Latina

Latin single women are some of the most sensual people in the world. Not only are Latinas beautiful, but they convey sensuality with their fluid movements. If you have met a Latin single woman who you would like to date, you may wonder what cultural differences there are that you should know about.

First of all, Latin single women have grown up in a large extended family. She may be closer to her third cousin twice removed than you are to your brother. Not only are nuclear families larger, but Hispanics often have grandparents, uncles, and nephews living with them.

Her family is going to be very important to her, and if the relationship is going to go anywhere, she will want their stamp of approval. You need to be prepared to spend a significant amount of time at family gatherings and extend your charm to members of the whole family.

More than likely, the Latin single women you meet will be overwhelmingly Catholic. Unlike white Catholics, Hispanics take the religion quite seriously, including the Vatican's edicts on sex and contraception. This does not mean that your Latina lover won't sleep with you. But it does mean that she will feel guilty about it.

If you are dating a Hispanic woman, you should consider going to church with her from time to time. It will give you a window into a belief system, not to mention please her enormously. When you first meet Latin single women, you will be surprised at how physically affectionate they are. You shouldn't misinterpret this as being open to sexual advances. Hispanic culture has different boundaries when it comes to hugging and kissing, but that doesn't mean that she is ready to jump into bed with you.

One of the best dates you can take Latin single women out on is dinner and dancing. Dancing is very important in Hispanic culture and she will probably be very interested in all kinds of dance. Another good date is a simple walk. Traditional courtship in many Latin American countries involves walking around the town circle with a potential suitor.

When you meet Latin single women, you may notice that they will make good wives. They are trained to put men's needs first. They will also be likely to see you as a good catch as you are more attentive to their needs than Hispanic men typically are.

One caution though, when reading this article, you may get the sense that all Latin single women are the same. Not only are all individuals different, but there are many cultures within Latin American society. A third generation Latina will probably be more acculturated to American customs than someone who just immigrated here.

Further, Latin America is a big place – bigger than Europe in fact. Just as you wouldn't think that someone from Britain was the same as someone from Poland or that women in Sweden and Spain were the same, you shouldn't assume that Latin America is a monolithic culture.

When you want to meet Latin single women, you should get to know as much about their culture and their individual tastes as you can.

24. How to Date Latin Women

Are you interested in Latin women? Dating a Latina requires you to develop a certain cultural sensitivity.

First of all, you should realize that the world south of the American border is a very big place. A woman from Brazil is likely to have different cultural traditions than a woman of Mexican heritage.

Think about it from a European standpoint. Europe is much smaller geographically from Latin America, but the regional differences are stark. You would expect a woman from Russia to have different expectations than a woman from Italy, who in turn would be different from a British woman. Latin America is no different.

Get to know Latin American culture, geography and politics. Know the difference between Uruguay and Paraguay. It also helps if you make an attempt to learn Spanish or Portuguese.

But, don't think that every Latina speaks the same kind of Spanish. In Mexico, a burrito is a food with beans and rice. In Argentina, it is a little donkey.

If you are interested in Latin women, dating customs may be somewhat different. Latin women are, by and large, Catholic, and may be more traditional and conservative than their white counterparts.

Latin women dating are more likely to take their Catholic faith seriously than white Catholic women. That means, they take the Vatican's dictates about birth control and other sexual matters quite seriously.

If you are dating a Latina woman, you need to put on your dancing shoes. The Latin American culture is very open to all kinds of dancing, and she will expect you to be able to tear up the floor.

Latin culture is very romantic. You will be expected to romance the Latin woman you are dating. Bring her flowers, pepper her with endearments, and wine and dine her. Put some effort into the relationship and she will reciprocate.

Latinas place strong emphasis on their families. It is not unusual for your girlfriend to be closer to a second cousin than you are to your brother. The extended family has strong roots in the Latin culture, so you will need to expand what your definition of family is.

A Latina may also have more traditional ideas than her white sisters about what men and women's roles in the family are. They have been raised in a macho culture. Even if they say they want to break this mold, many Latin women dating white men subconsciously expect their dates to fall into this pattern.

If you are with a Latin woman, dating leads to courtship, and courtship leads to marriage. The courtship of a Latin woman involves paying attention to many traditional norms.

For instance, a woman of Mexican heritage may expect her man to walk on the street side of the sidewalk when escorting her in order to protect her from the traffic. As you get to know your Latina girlfriend, you will learn the types of things she expects from you.

If you are going to pursue Latin women, dating becomes a multicultural experience. Embrace the richness and variety of the Latin American culture.

25. Dating Tips on Dating Sexy Latin Women

Are you dating or interested in dating a sexy Latin woman? If so then you might need to learn a little bit about her culture.

The Latin American population is very big and covers a big area. Just like women from Russia have a different culture than women from Italy, so do the various Latin cultures differ. A woman from

Mexico will have different cultural traditions than a woman from Brazil.

When you think about the different countries within Europe, remember that Europe is much smaller than Latin America and yet the cultural difference between European countries is huge. It is the same with the different cultures throughout Latin America; they will all differ quite a bit in their traditions and beliefs.

If you are going to date a Latin woman you will need to know which part of Latin America she is from and learn about her

culture and politics. You might even want to learn to speak her language if she speaks Spanish or Portuguese.

Even the language will differ from one part of the country to another. For example, in Argentina a burrito is a little donkey, whereas in Mexico it is a food with rice and beans.

The dating customs might also be very different from what your dating customs are. Latin people are often Catholic and so they might have very conservative dating customs.

Latin women are more serious about their religion than many white women are and so they can be very traditional and conservative when it comes to dating. They can be quite serious about the Catholic views on sex before marriage and birth control. Although this does not mean they will not be interested in a sexual relationship, but they might be much more conservative.

Do you like to dance? If you aren't much of a dancer then you better start learning because Latina women love to dance. The Latin American society loves dancing and will participate in all kinds of dancing, so put on your dancing shoes if you are dating a Latina woman.

Latin women also love romance and Latin men are very romantic. So to keep with the Latin tradition you will need to learn how to be romantic. Send or bring her flowers, take her out for a romantic dinner or a romantic stroll along the beach.

Latin Americans are also very family orientated so you won't just be dating the woman but all of her extended family too.

Expect to spend a lot of time with her parents, brothers and sisters, grandparents and even aunts, uncles, nieces and nephews. The family has strong roots in Latin culture and you will want her family's stamp of approval for your relationship to work.

Latin Americans are very cultural so you will need to adapt to their traditions if you want a long term relationship with a Latin woman. They have traditional ideas about men and women's roles in the home. They might have traditional expectations for things like a man walking on the street side of the sidewalk and opening and closing the car door for her.

So if you are dating a Latina woman and would like the relationship to become a long term one then learn her culture and embrace her family and their traditions and you will have a happy, fulfilled relationship.

26. How to Meet Beautiful Chinese Women

If you are interested in meeting beautiful Chinese women to date and maybe marry, the good news is that the internet has made the whole process much less complicated than it used to be. There are hundreds of online dating sites where you can sign up, fill out a profile and be matched with the girl of your dreams.

Before you dive right in though, you should take some time to check out several different sites. Each site will have its own terms of service which will include all the fees associated with using the site. It's also important to note what type of information you will need to include in a profile. If you want to meet someone special it's important that everyone on the site has a complete profile. Otherwise how will you know who might be a match and who isn't?

To find a great online dating site, ask around to friends and family. You may be surprised at the number of people you know who have found true love online. A personal recommendation is always a great resource. Also you can ask around in online forums associated with online dating for some recommendations.

When you find a great site to help you find your Chinese lady, make sure that you fill out your profile completely and honestly. You are hoping to meet this woman in person at some point so it

doesn't do you any good to lie on your profile. If you do, she will be very disappointed when she meets you since she was expecting someone else and the last thing you want to see when you meet her is a look of disappointment on her face.

Try to learn some of her language before the two of you meet. That will make getting to know each other so much easier. It's also important to keep in mind that not all Chinese women are the same. That may sound dumb, but when dealing with foreign cultures it's easy to stereotype them. Just like not all American women are the same, no two Chinese women will be exactly the same either. Try to keep your preconceived notions to a minimum.

Oh, and one last thing, be very careful about avoiding scams. Unfortunately even on dating sites, there can be scammers. Never, ever send money to anyone you meet no matter how pathetic a story you're being told. It does happen occasionally that someone will sign up to one of these sites, they may be a woman or they may just pretend to be a woman, in the hopes of creating an online relationship with a man only to lure him into sending her money. This is rare, but it can happen so don't ever send money to anyone. Period.

Meeting beautiful Chinese women is easier than ever thanks to the internet. Just keep these tips in mind as you dip your toe into the online dating world. If you do, you will greatly improve your odds of meeting Miss Right.

27. Dating Black Singles

Know the Keys to Black Dating Success

For quite some time now, people of all ethnic backgrounds have relied on the old traditional ways as their first path to dating. This is as true of the black dating community as any other ethnic group, but some have wondered if singles in the African-American community have been as quick to embrace the latest in dating technology. History tells us that many tight-knit ethnic groups such as those of Hispanic and African-American background are more reliant on traditions when it comes to meeting and finding a suitable mate for a long-term relationship. That means that meeting other singles who are new to the black dating scene can be difficult, but these days there seems to be more of a push to get some of those whose backgrounds are more tied to tradition in dating to accept the opportunity to use the online medium to enhance their prospects.

There was a time when those of strong ethnic heritage might resist the idea of turning to technology to help their dating efforts, but times and technology have been changing more rapidly than some want to admit. While some in the black dating community may regret the change, others are looking at this as a change for the better.

Let's face it, whether you're new to black dating or not, choosing someone who is compatible with you is something that can be difficult and fraught with potential mistakes. Of course, online dating sites and new technology offering alternatives to black dating singles don't minimize the chance that someone will go wrong. We can say with fair certainty that meeting someone online is not necessarily easier than meeting people offline in the "real world" with really one exception: those who have turned to online technology can at least be sure that the people they meet online are more than likely there because they've faced the same challenges. That point, at least, gives a potential relationship established online a leg up on the all-important "something in common" aspect of a new relationship.

Whether those who are active in the black dating community are turning more to tradition or more toward online dating opportunities, the same rules apply. Find other interested singles who are looking for a solid match, make sure you have things in common, get to know one another a bit before you start to actually date (in the online world, e-mails are a great way to get to know someone), and take care when you begin a new relationship. In all of those ways, the black dating community is exactly the same as any other, but they also have the advantage of having a supportive, tradition-rich history to help lay a solid foundation for their new potential romance. So what is it that you're waiting for?

28. How to Meet Asian Women

If meeting Asian women is something you're interested in doing, you're in luck. There are more online resources than ever before that will allow you to meet, and maybe marry, the woman of your dreams. Even though this process is easier than ever before, it's not without its risks. There are some simple things you need to be on the lookout for so you can be sure that your online dating will bring you happiness and not heartache.

When you meet someone on an online dating site it allows both of you the opportunity to meet many other people, and narrow the field down to 'the one'. That would be virtually impossible to do just by taking your chances locally. You can also go slowly and take your time getting to know one another, since all of your meetings are happening either online or on the phone, neither of you has to worry about things getting physical too quickly. That means that you are much more likely to build a really deep and lasting bond and not get confused into thinking that your physical attraction is really love.

When trying to decide on which online dating site you want to join, narrow your choices down to a few websites that are offering what you are looking for. For example, some online dating sites are geared to singles who just want to have a casual fling. If you are looking for a serious long term relationship, that type of site obviously wouldn't be your best choice.

Also take the time to carefully read the terms of service before signing up to an online dating site. You want to make sure you know how much it will cost and if there are going to be any additional fees down the line. Having an idea of how they screen, or if they screen, their members is also a good thing to know. Even if they say that all of their members are carefully screened you still have to be careful of any red flags when you meet someone. Ultimately your online safety is your responsibility.

When you create your profile try to be very specific about what types of things you like, what you don't like, and what you are looking for in a woman. You want to be as detailed as possible, without giving out any potentially dangerous information such as addresses, phone numbers, etc. You should also include a few pictures in your profile. Make sure they are current and accurately represent the way you look now.

You do want to put your best foot forward, but you don't want to be misleading. After all, when you meet someone special online, you'll eventually want to meet her offline and that won't work out very well if you've misrepresented yourself in any way. Be honest.

It doesn't happen that often, but it does happen, sometimes scammers will sign up to a dating site and fill out a profile all with the express purpose of luring gullible men, and women, into sending them money. If someone you meet online starts asking for money that should be considered a huge red flag. Con artists will 'make' you fall in love with them so they can play on that love all in an effort to separate you from your money. Don't give anyone money online.

Meeting Asian women online makes the process much easier than if you tried to find the right women by chance. Just make sure that as you open your heart, you keep your wallet closed.

29. How to Understand Women

Do you sometimes have a hard time understanding women? How do they act and how do they think? Does it sometimes seem like they are from another planet? Well, let me give you some advice to help you out in understanding women and people in general.

The first mistake you're making is expecting her to think like you and be like you. You expect her to see the world as you do. This is a big mistake! She will never be like you or think like you. She will not be a clone of you.

We are all unique individuals and not alike. It would be a pretty boring world if we were all alike and thought alike. We all have different opinions of things and see the world differently based upon our upbringing, experiences, knowledge, etc.

And don't make the mistake of trying to change a woman that you are dating into someone like yourself. Sorry, it just won't happen. Accept her unconditionally with her faults and all.

People are resistant to change and if you're constantly trying to change her, you are just going to end up alienating her.

So in closing, remember this: Any woman you meet will not exactly think like you and be like you. If you can accept this statement it will go a long way in helping you to understand women and people in general.

30. Relax To Win Love Back

There are many different ways that you can win love back, but the key is to begin with the basics. If you try to win love back, you are going to need to have a solid game plan coupled with a solid sense of confidence. Every relationship has ups, downs and unique challenges, and a different strategy is going to be necessary for each individual situation. There is no real right or wrong answer set in stone when it comes to trying to rekindle a relationship. Every relationship is going to come with its own unique challenges, and you need to come up with your own unique strategy for rekindling the relationship based on your own situation, rather than necessarily based upon the advice of others.

Even if you have friends, family members or other acquaintances that have been through similar situations, the solution they found in order to win love back may not necessarily work for you. This is because there are always underlying causes and other situations that come into play that may not necessarily have come into play in the other relationships. One of the things that you need to consider when you are ready to win love back is that desperate behavior will repel your lost love rather than allow you to rekindle things or attract them back. You need to take the time to identify the problems that broke the relationship up, and you need to begin crafting a solution accordingly in order to win love back rather than repelling it further. The best way to approach the situation when you are ready to win love back is to start at the beginning. Work hard and prove yourself like you did when you first met him or her. One of the most common mistakes that is made when it comes to trying to win back love is focusing on everything that went wrong rather than trying to focus on the good things that made the relationship strong in the first place. Change the situation, start fresh, and you will be able to win love back even when it feels hopeless or like a lost cause.

If you are placing any undue restrictions on your lover or spouse, now is the time to let them go. Don't put restrictions on your love, or they may find themselves resisting you, which will undo your hard work and progress when it comes to rekindling the relationship and learning how to win back love. Now is the time to let tensions slide and focus on the positive nature of the relationship. What drew you to your significant other, and what drew them to you? Focus on these good things and let the bad and negative feelings slide away. Once you can prove yourself again, learning how to win love back will be easier than ever.

31. Goal Setting System for Scoring With Women:

Goal-setting is a powerful system in getting what you want, and this is, scoring with hot & sexy beautiful women. "As you think, so you become." If you focus on a goal with determination, backed with a burning desire, you'll experience it. Setting a goal to meet and pick up women is acknowledging to your conscious and subconscious minds that where you stand as far as scoring with women is not where you want to be. Having a goal creates positive pressure on yourself, which is necessary to move you forward and motivate you to pick up women.

Now, I will explain the following steps to goal-setting to meet and pick up women.

Step 1- The first step in goal-setting is desire. Desire is the great motivator, the powerful force that drives you toward your goal.
Step 2- The second step is belief - you must believe with all your heart and no doubts that you have the ability to achieve your goal.
Step 3 - The third and most important step is to write your goal of meeting and picking up women in complete detail, exactly as you wish to have it. Until your goal is committed to paper by you, it is not a goal; it is simply a wish backed by perhaps a lot of sexual fantasies.
Step 4 - The fourth step is to determine all the benefits you will receive by achieving your goals of scoring with women. Write out on paper all the benefits you will enjoy by accomplishing your goal. You should really enjoy this step. Just let your imagination run wild and put it on paper.
Step 5 - Step number five is to set a deadline- decide exactly when you are going to accomplish your goal of picking up women and put it on paper.
Step 6 - Step number six is to identify the obstacles you will have to overcome to achieve your goal of picking up women. You will discover that any major obstacles lingering in your mind and preventing you from picking up women will become small when you write them down on paper.
Step 7 - Step number seven is to clearly define the knowledge you need to learn in order to accomplish your goal.
Step 8 - Step number eight is to take all the details that you have identified in step 6 and 7 and make a plan. Be sure and make it complete in every little detail, with all the things you need to do to accomplish your goal.

Step 9 - Step number nine is to get a clear mental picture of your goal as already attained. Picture in your mind over and over seeing yourself scoring and picking up women. Just let your imagination run wild. Become completely obsessed with picking up women in your mind.

Step 10 - Your final step is to back your plan with determination, persistence, and a burning desire to never, never give up until you have achieved your goal.

Here's an example of a written goal: By _____(insert date) I will pick up and score with a hot & sexy beautiful woman. I am now going out often and pursuing a relationship with women by every means possible until this goal is accomplished. I'm now taking action when I see an opportunity to pick up a woman. When I go to clubs now, I don't just sit there being passive and just watch other men meet and pick up women. I'm aggressive with women now and move into action quickly and easily. It is extremely easy now for me to meet and talk with women, get their phone number, date, seduce and become intimate with women.

Signed_____(your name) Date _____

This is just an example of what to write for your goal. You can write whatever you want, this is just a guideline. This is very important. Write your goal on a 8 1/2 x 11 piece of paper, preferably blank with no lines. Now, you need to get copies of the popular womens' magazines featuring pretty women. Cut out pictures of the pretty models and paste them all around your written goal.

When reading your goal look at these pictures and visualize yourself picking up women.

Looking at these pictures will work on your subconscious mind and motivate you to reach your goal. Read your goal and look at the photos twice daily. Once when you get up in the morning and once when you go to bed. These are the best times to do this because your subconscious mind is more receptive to suggestions at this time.

Additional Tips To Help You Achieve Your Goals

1. Focus all of your attention, desire and energy in accomplishing your goal at hand. Forget completely about any consequences of failure with women. Remember that you usually get what you think about most.

2. When you start on your goal, concentrate all of your energy without any distractions on the successful completion of your goal. Make reaching your goal an all-consuming obsession.

3. Develop a self-talk vocabulary to reach your goal of scoring with women. Make it a habit to repeat again and again to yourself, "I want to - I can" in regards to scoring with women.

4. Substitute the word "Try" with the word "Will" in your vocabulary associated with scoring with women. This is a form of semantics and creates a new attitude of concentrating on things that you "Will do," instead of things you plan to "Try," with a built-in excuse in advance for possible failure.

5. Substitute the word "Can't" with the word "Can" in your daily vocabulary too. Always tell yourself you "Can" do things you set your mind to.

In conclusion, set your goals and go for it! Happy Hunting!

32. Proven Ways of Mending a Broken Heart

The best part about being a human, is the ability to actually deeply care about and love someone. To be in love is probably one of the greatest emotions we can experience. When you're in a relationship and everything is going well, it's sometimes easy to take the relationship for granted. Unfortunately, relationships, even the ones you thought were going smoothly, can come to an abrupt end. While truly caring about someone and loving them is great and a source of pleasure, when the relationship is over it can be a huge source of pain, sorrow, and a broken heart. If the break up is recent, you may not believe it, but there are things you can do to begin mending a broken heart.

Unfortunately, there is no magic pill, potion, lotion, or method for instantly mending a broken heart. It is imperative that you understand this. After a break up, there will be times when your emotions are going to be up, down, sideways, diagonal, and every other way, but right. In fact, you'll probably experience combinations of emotions you never thought possible. One example is anger and sadness mixed together. You'll find that sometimes your emotions can change at the drop of a hat. You'll be feeling fine, laughing one minute, the next you'll be really sad, even crying. The most important thing you have to realize is that it all seems bleak and dark now. However, as time presses on, things will get better.

It is critical that you try to reign in your emotions. Does this mean you should bottle up your emotions? No, absolutely not. However, it does mean that you shouldn't let your sadness, anger, depression, or any other emotion control you for long periods of time. If you're feeling sad, allow yourself to have a "pity party" for a maximum of 15 minutes. Then, say to yourself "Okay, that's enough. It's time to stop.

Mending a broken heart is also going to require you to try and stay

busy. If you give your mind a lot of idle time to think, it will probably want to think about your break up. This isn't good. Try to

keep your mind and body active. You probably won't feel like doing this very much, but it's important. Go somewhere, do something, try to drag friends along. Tell them to not let you talk about the break up. Try not to sit around the house and do nothing. That's the worst thing you can do.

33. After You Breakup How to Get Over Someone You Love

You have just gone through a big break up and you are asking yourself how to get over someone you love. There are a few steps you can do to help get over your lost love and move on. These steps are made to remind you why things got to where they are and use that to remind yourself.

Your first solution of how to get over someone is to remind yourself of all of the times you were treated like a second class situation in the relationship. Ask yourself if that sort of abuse is what you want back. The obvious answer of "no" will reinforce the breakup and weaken feelings of love that might be lingering.

Figuring out how to get over someone you love does not have to be difficult. When your feelings of love arise, redirect them towards others in your life. Focus the love you are feeling now to where it is most important. The positive elements that are currently in your life will provide the foundation for getting over your lost love. You are important and worth it.

You should also put your trust into the fact that things will improve. You have grown from your relationship. The things in our life that hurt us only serve to make us stronger. This is how you can learn how to get over someone you love, by taking in the lessons you have and using them to better yourself and your outlook.

Do not view your ex with bitterness, for that will infect you and make you hurt over the loss more. Instead, direct compassion towards the person you loved, because they will be hurting too. They will also be suffering through the loss. If they have moved on, then you should take that and use it to help you move on.

How to get over someone you love involves taking the passion that you still have, and redirecting it into other aspects of your life. There is an incredible amount of power behind it and if you let it linger on the person you used to love, it will ruin you. If you instead take it and turn it into the driving force that empowers you to become better and achieve happiness.

Always be sure to remind yourself of why you broke up. There had to be pain and misery and strong emotions that brought about the end of your relationship. When you start to want for your ex again, remind yourself why you left them, and realize that you deserve so much more. You deserve happiness and joy and lingering on the pain is not how to get over someone you love.

You are important and you need to be able to move on. Focusing on the bad things will not help you to move on and find love and happiness again. How to get over someone you love is about redirecting your love and passion into becoming better.

Falling in love is usually the easy part. Mending a broken heart is not. That's just one of the cruel realities of life. Everything has an equal and an opposite. The wonderful, uplifting, feelings you get from being in love, are the exact opposite to the miserable, depression and sadness that go along with a break up. Time, an active lifestyle, happy thoughts, and good friends will get you through this tough time.

Where to Take a Date

34. Free Dating Women Ideas – No Cost Dates that Will Impress the Ladies

Do you need free dating women ideas? In fact, many of the most romantic dates you can take your lady out on won't cost you a dime. This article will show you 10 free dating women options that give you not cost dates that will still impress the ladies.

What is one of a woman's most persistent romantic fantasies? That would have to be a long walk on a moonlit beach. In personal ad after personal ad, you see this wish appear. So, why not make it a part of your free dating women repartee? She will be far more impressed than if you took her to a fancy French restaurant?

If you are doing a daytime date, consider going on a bike ride together. Ride for a while. Stop and have a picnic. Then ride home. The exercise will do you wonders and there's a sense of having shared space without having to fill it with words.

Most towns have free concerts from time to time, but particularly in the summer months. These range from classical music played by symphonies to patriotic tunes by a military band, to popular music. A concert tells your date that you have a touch of class and in no way screams "cheap."

Similarly, most museums have at least one evening a month designated as a free or donation only night. Take advantage of this and your date will think you have some culture.

Plan a picnic for your date. You don't have to get imported Cheese or fancy wine either. But, do take the time to make the food special. Cut off the crusts on the bread or make a nice desert. Fruits such as strawberries are easy to pack and quite sexy at the same time.

Another free dating women idea is to volunteer to babysit a married couple's children. Not only is it fun to play with the rugrats, it gives your date the idea that you could be good with kids in the future. This will make her think more romantically toward you.

Along the same lines, go "house shopping." (Make sure you are only looking at homes well outside your means though so she

doesn't get any ideas.) Again, this has her thinking toward the future which may make you happy in the present.

There are also seasonal things that you can do that make good free dating women events. For instance, at Halloween, carve pumpkins. There is something very charming about carving funny faces in a gourd. You will probably have more fun doing this than you would if you spent money on a movie.

The next idea I have is also holiday related. Go out and look at Christmas lights. People spend a lot of time and money competing for the distinction of having the best holiday decorations outside their home. You can take advantage of this entertainment for free!

My final free dating woman tip is to build a large fire in your fireplace and read poetry to each other. If that doesn't get her in the mood, nothing ever will.

35. Some of the Best Places to Take a Date

It seems as though there are two main times when it's tough to think of just the right type of date for you and your partner: when the relationship is really young and you don't know each other's

tastes very well, and when the relationship is a little older and you get stuck in a rut. For any time when it seems like you just can't think of the best dating ideas, here are some simple tips that might be able to jump start your imagination.

This may be difficult advice to follow, but if you can, you'll be much more relaxed and have more fun on your date: don't take it too seriously. Dates are supposed to be fun times shared with you and someone special. It doesn't have to be on some timetable or schedule. Just try to think of something that you and your partner would find fun and will help the two of you create a deeper bond and some lasting memories.

Simple things can be great for the first date such as a picnic, watching a sunset, etc. These things will be a relaxing and romantic date and will allow the two of you plenty of time to talk and get to know each other better.

You can also do dinner and a movie and even though this isn't the most unique of dates it can still be a great way to spend time together, especially if there is a movie that both of you are interested in. This type of date isn't as conducive to talking, though of course you'll talk over dinner, but that may be a good thing if you're a little shy and this is one of the first dates you've had with your partner.

Going to a carnival or a festival is a great date for summertime. This type of date is another great option for a casual first date. It will allow a lot of distractions in case the conversation starts to wane. There will always be something or someone the two of you can talk about.

If you go on a date to a place that serves alcohol, if you're an adult, make sure you don't drink too much. This may sound like obvious advice but drinking too much is an easy mistake to make when you're nervous. If you drink too much and become belligerent or a sloppy drunk, it will likely be your last date with that person. This is a point I can't stress enough. Don't over drink!

Another good piece of date advice is to make sure you have a conversation with your partner, not a lecture. It's important that you let your partner talk too, ask a little about them, don't just spend the whole time talking about yourself or your interests. Again, it's easy to talk too much when you're nervous, but if you do then it can be a real turn off and you most likely won't see that person again any time soon. Make sure you give and take when it comes to the conversation. This is a wonderful opportunity to get to really know the other person on a deeper level. That is the basis for any strong, fun, loving relationship.

These are the best dating ideas and they can help you not only plan a great date, but also have fun and make a great impression on your date. Just keep them in mind and you'll be much better at dating and have more dates and more fun.

36. Golf Dating

Do any of you guys play golf? If you, do have you ever considered taking a date to a golf driving range to hit a few balls? Most single women don't play golf, but most would be willing to give it a try with a little coaxing.

The reason I'm writing about a golf date has a special meaning and advantage for you. Being that most likely your date does not know how to play golf, you will be able to be her teacher!

What's great about this is that there will be a lot of physical contact while teaching her to hit the ball. You will have your arms around her from behind showing her how to grip and swing the club. This can be a very erotic experience for you if you know what I mean! I don't know about you, but I just love the feeling of my crotch up against a woman's butt, even with clothes on.

If you don't have your own set of golf clubs, that's no problem. A lot of driving ranges and golf courses with driving ranges have clubs available for rent.

So in closing guys, consider going on a date to the driving range. It's a lot of fun!

37. More Dating Ideas

1. AIR SHOW – If you have an annual air show near you. By all means don't pass this up for a fantastic dating idea.

2. AMUSEMENT PARKS -This really makes for a fun date, especially if you both enjoy thrill-seeking rides such as roller coasters, etc. Also, don't forget to try and win her a teddy bear or other keepsake.

3. ANNUAL EVENTS – Most of your larger towns and cities offer many annual events and are great places to go on a date. These events include festivals, chili cook-offs, firework displays, contests, ethnic festivals, sporting tournaments, arts & craft shows, horse shows, concerts, fairs, etc.

4. ANTIQUES -Most women like antiques and they would really enjoy looking at them and shopping for them.

5. ARCHERY RANGES -Remember when you were a kid and played bows and arrows? Well, now you can do it for real with real bows and arrows. Check your area out for indoor and outdoor archery ranges where you and your date can shoot to your heart's content. Who knows, just maybe Cupid will hit you both with his arrow. .

6. **ART GALLERIES** -This is a great idea for a unique and real interesting date. Discover the beautiful world of art. You both will certainly have more of an appreciation for art after touring a few galleries.

7. **AUTO SHOWS** -I think there's a little bit of new car fever in all of us and even if we can't afford a new car/truck we still like to look at them and dream. This is a most enjoyable experience to share with a date.

8. **BALLOON RIDES** -I am referring to hot-air balloon rides. This is a breath-taking experience you both will never forget. It's very romantic and some rides even come with champagne.

9. **BASEBALL BATTING CAGES** -I'm sure you've probably seen these fenced in cages where a machine throws balls at you and you hit them with a bat. This is a real fun and challenging thing to do to test your batting skills.

10. **BAZAARS** -Bazaars are a real fun thing to do and feature a variety of food, entertainment, crafts, plants, auctions, fun & games for children, jewelry, antiques, home-baked goods, prizes, games, clothes, bingo, and refreshments. So, if you're looking for something different to do to break the monotony, go to these bazaars on a date.

11. **BEACH OR LAKE** -This is one of my favorite places to take a date, especially at night: There's nothing more romantic than taking a moonlight stroll along the beach or lake.

12. **BEACH HOUSE RENTAL** -Great for getting away from the hectic life in the city for some rest and relaxation.

38. Dating Tip for Shy Guys

Reading up on dating tips for shy guys can certainly help you make a good impression on your next date. And don't forget that these dating tips are not just for the shy person going out for the first time. They can help you even if you're experienced in dating, because it's easy to forget the basics.

A good tip to remember is not to try to go overboard. She's not going to expect you to take her to a restaurant that's going to cost you $100 on your first date. And if she does expect that, you might be better off asking someone else out on a date.

She also shouldn't expect you to take her on a date that is overly complicated. Keeping it simple is best, especially for first date. Go for things that are fun and unusual and that will be memorable for her. Go to one of those pizza parlors with the characters in the video games that are usually thought of as being places for little kids. Go to the zoo and buy her cotton candy.

Amusement parks and carnivals are great places for dates. Everybody likes to be a kid now and then. So going to a place like this and riding rides let you be silly for awhile.

Don't forget to play the bottle toss of the ring toss and try to win her prize. Winning your girl a stuffed animal is something that will be great on a date for years to come.

Don't see an overly serious movie on your first date. Going to see a very heavy show about an historical figure might not be great for first date. But don't feel you have to go and see the latest, greatest "date movie."

Choose a movie that's more neutral than that for a first date. Go see the latest cartoon movie that's popular for kids and have a silly time. It can be fun to laugh at the things you used to like as a little kid and you may find the movie's really great anyway.

Choosing fun and quirky things like this can let her see that you just want to have a good time. It can help set her at ease and make her less nervous, which will in turn make you less nervous, too.

If it's clear to her that you just really want to enjoy yourself, that's going to impress her. If she can tell you're not out to try to impress her with an expensive date or trying to be someone you're not, she'll notice.

Don't forget to pay her a compliment, too. It can be easy to forget, especially if you're nervous. But find something that you like whether it's her perfume, her clothes or her sense of humor and say something nice about it. She'll be able to relax because she'll be less worried about impressing you.

Don't forget these dating tips for shy guys next time you're ready to ask someone out.

39. Personality Dating - Contemporary Tips and Advantages

In a world of ever evolving technology, the possibility of measuring and finding a perfect match for yourself is becoming more and more possible. Some would even dare to say that this capability is already here. Enter personality dating! There are a few ways you can enter this arena, and when done right, can yield awesome results in your dating life. You might even find the person you are looking for.

There are several personality types in the dating world, and in the world in general. The most common are passive, assertive and aggressive. You can find out which one you are by taking a couple of personality tests, or you probably already know which one you are. You can find some of these tests online, or even at some professional dating websites. The most balanced personality to have is an assertive one. This is not too passive and not too aggressive. Rather, you are attentive to what the other person is saying, you are sensitive to their viewpoints, and are also inquisitive to the point that sparks healthy conversation between the both of you. A great way to find out if you are being assertive is if during the course of a phone conversation, both you and your partner have equal opportunities and chances to speak to each other, and both of your talk times are about the same.

Personality tests are quite essential in personality dating because they essentially find out what kind of person you are. The Keirsey Temperament test is a famous one to take. Also the Jung Personality Test, the Big Five personality tests and the Meyers Briggs Personality Tests are famous ones to take. Each of these tests will give you a small snapshot of your personality type. The results can change or remain the same throughout the course of your life, depending on what kind of person you are developing into at that present time.

When it comes to online dating sites searches, this is where personality dating comes into full force. The dating sites use your results from your personality tests to match against people from all over the nation. Remember to keep your geographic options open because you could very well be missing out on a perfect personality match that is a few states away. The possibilities are endless when it comes to this, and there are plenty of success stories out there to get you going.

40. Advice for First Dates

There are some things that you must never, never talk about on a first date. If you do, you're taking a major risk of turning off your date and spoiling your chances of ever getting a second date.

Don't talk about the following topics on your first date:

Do you have any mental, financial, legal, or divorce problems? If you do, keep it to yourself. Don't share these personal problems with your date.

Don't talk about your bad luck with dating women. A real turn off would be to make a statement such as, "All the women I date turn out to be bitches."

Don't discuss any previous relationships and express bitterness towards relationships that didn't work out.

Don't jump the gun and start talking about future dates together. The only purpose of the first date is to get to know each other and not to plan a future together. If you start talking about doing things together so soon, she's going to feel pressured and perhaps intimidated.

Don't ever assume that just because she agreed to go on a first date with you that it will lead to a quick relationship. Take things slow and don't rush her into a relationship. Establish a strong friendship first and romance will follow.

41. **How to Flirt Effectively**

Men and women flirt differently, for different reasons and expect different outcomes to the flirting. However, if you put aside that outcome and flirt just to be friendly you are opening yourself to different opportunities. You may well end up with a new lover but if that doesn't work out you could meet someone who becomes a good friend and who knows who she might introduce you to. Keep your options open.

After you have exchanged glances and smiles across a room and you are fairly confident that SHE thinks that she might like to get to know you better, send a drink to her. But remember that ALL you are buying is a drink. Don't expect her to fall at your feet. Sometimes it is nice just to send someone a drink, watch when she receives it and smile, then look away – look back again later to show your interest.

If you find yourself invited to her table, keep your mind on the conversation and not on getting a date with her. Most women want to know what kind of person they are going out with long before they actually go out with them. Make an effort to get to know her and give her the opportunity to get to know you before diving in for a date.

Do not ever approach two women in the same group. No woman wants to feel like second best. Refrain from approaching one after another in the same group. You look like a loser and the women may think you are desperate and looking for any port in a storm. Even if you are, don't show it.

When you compliment a woman make certain that it is a genuine compliment. There's nothing worse than someone giving out a load

of overblown lines. Everyone has something great about them, notice that and compliment them genuinely.

Do not ever put your hands on a woman uninvited. Some women have no objection to 'touchy feely' encounters, others are horrified by it. Respect the person until you have had the opportunity to know more about her. Touching can be a lovely flirty action, but should be confined to the arms or resting the hand just above the arms and NOT touching, until you know more. Test the personal space by moving closer, noticing the reactions then moving back a little to remove the threat.

Respect yourself at all times. Women always fall for men who are that little bit unreachable. Don't hover or grovel or act desperate. Think of yourself as special and know what you deserve the very best.

42. How To Move On After relationship Failure

It's very easy to cling to a relationship and convince yourself that you'll never find anyone as special as your partner again. This is actually a normal part of the grieving process when you are going through a painful end to a relationship. Everyone is different and everyone has to find the path that works best for them, but here are some ideas of how to move on after relationships that tend to work well for many people.

The first thing that you have to understand is that whatever went wrong in your past relationship doesn't have to be repeated in your next one. If you would like to have a better outcome the next time around, you owe it to yourself to spend some time analyzing the problems that you had in your past relationship, especially the things that you did wrong.

In order to avoid repeating the same mistakes again, try to make changes in yourself and the way you deal with things. For example, if part of the problem with your past relationship was the fact that every time your partner tried to talk to you about how they were feeling you'd get mad and defensive, make sure you can change the behavior before you meet someone new.

What's the point of going out and finding someone else to love if you're just going to do the same destructive behaviors all over again? It's likely that you'll just cause you and your new partner a lot of pain. Instead, take some time to make yourself the best version of you that you can be and you'll have a much better chance of your next relationship working out much better.

It's also important for you to take a long hard look at the traits your ex had that you didn't like or didn't get along with. Try not to just go out and find someone with those same traits. I know this may sound like a no brainer, but we tend to be attracted to the same basic types of people over and over again. If you don't recognize this you may actually find another partner that was a lot like your ex and you'll repeat the same pattern over again.

And last, but not least, allow yourself all the time you need. It's very common for family and friends to encourage you to start dating again, even before you think you're really ready. Don't allow yourself to be pressured in to start dating too soon. It's not good for you and it won't be good for anyone you meet if you still haven't gotten over your ex. Take your time, you'll know when you're ready.

Having a relationship end is one of life's toughest challenges. Just never forget that you can find another love if you follow these tips on how to move on after relationships. Don't give up on your chance to be happy, just keep your heart open and you can find the love of your life... again.

43. How to Stop a Break Up

The test of true love is how long two people stay together; no matter what life throws at them. Sometimes, a mature relationship can struggle. It is at this point that a decision has to be made. More often than not, the decision to break up is the most common one made. If you believe your relationship is rocky and may be heading toward a breakup, but you're not ready to throw in the towel yet, you need to know how to stop a breakup.

There are many reasons why people break up. Most breakups happen because the relationship has grown stale. One person, or sometimes both people, in a relationship realize that they just don't seem to have anything in common with the other person anymore. Maybe the spark of attraction is gone. Maybe they feel that there is someone else out there better for them. If your partner already broke it off with you, then you know the reason, or reasons, why they didn't want to continue in the relationship with you. However, it's much easier to stop a breakup before it happens.

If you believe your relationship is heading toward a breakup or your significant other has broken it off with you, and you're not quite ready to give up yet. If you think your relationship is worth fighting for. Whether or not it truly is, can only be determined by you. Then read the following advice on how to stop a breakup; to see if it can help you.

Think things through. There's nothing worse than a knee-jerk reaction. When someone breaks up with you, it is very painful. All you think about is the positive within the other person. However, sometimes, a breakup can be a blessing in disguise. It helps if you can put down on a piece of paper the good things and the bad things about the other person.

Divide the paper in half. Write down all the positive attributes and qualities the other person possesses and then write down all the negative attributes and qualities the person possesses. Make sure that you do this when you're rational and clear thinking. Be honest with yourself. Don't sugar coat it. If the negative qualities and attributes outweigh the positive, then perhaps, there's no reason to want to stop the breakup.

Talk to your partner. Another piece of advice on how to stop a breakup is to talk to your partner. Let your significant other know what you are thinking. The relationship you are in with your partner is two-way. If you can have an honest discussion with your partner, you may be able to avoid a breakup.

They may be able to open up to you about something that is bothering them. It is very important that you don't get into any type of confrontation during the talk. If you do, you will only shut down their willingness to communicate with you. You need to listen and not become critical or angry. This may be hard to do, but it's very important.

Value love. It is not everyday in your life that you find a person who will love you as you are. If you think your partner loves you more than anything else, remember to value it. A little lack of excitement in the relationship is not proof that you have lost the connection. You might just have to rekindle the love embedded in the depths of your hearts. While your partner is with you, value the love you have for each other. In other words, don't take the other person for granted. In a mature relationship, taking someone for granted is very easy to do.

Get help from a professional. This is by far the best piece of advice on how to stop a breakup. If you truly cherish your relationship, and you seriously think that you're heading toward a breakup; then getting help from a professional is probably the best thing you can do. Therapists and relationship counselors have saved countless relationships. There's nothing to be embarrassed about if you have to resort to this. It's amazing how having a specially trained third party; who is completely neutral, listening to you and your partner discuss your problems can truly impact your relationship for the better.

44. Become A Challenge For Your Girlfriend

If you think your relationship is becoming stale and your girlfriend is getting bored with you then why not become a bit of a challenge for your girlfriend. Everyone likes a challenge so if you make some changes to make it a little more challenging you can bring the spark back into your relationship. If you give in to your girlfriends every need and are always at her beck and call then she may take it for granted and subconsciously even think you are a little weak. If you become a little less accommodating to her needs she may actually have more respect for you.

One good way to bring the spark back into the relationship is to try and act like the man you were at the start of the relationship. When relationships first start they are usually quite romantic and you probably gave her flowers and gifts or even write her little notes. These things happen less and less often as the relationship moves on and before you know it you never bring her flowers or gifts or write her notes. When a relationship reaches this stage you begin to take things for granted rather than seeing them as a very special lady.

If you take a look at your relationship and realize that this is what

has happened then you should take steps to rectify this. Start looking at your girlfriend the way you did at the beginning and start treating her like she is really special. If you begin doing these little special things like sending her flowers she will remember the guy that she fell in love with. This can bring back the spark in the relationship and you won't need to worry about trying to be a challenge for your girlfriend.

If your girlfriend seems to be drifting away, instinctively you may start to pull back too and then you both begin to drift apart. If this continues the relationship will fall into a downward spiral that will end badly. If she is drifting away then she is probably not happy and if you pull back that only makes her unhappier. Instead of pulling back, try to woo her again like you did when you first met her. She fell in love with you once and more than likely she wants that man back that she fell in love with.

To improve your relationship and get past this rut you need to go back to the guy you were at the beginning. The other thing you do need to consider is whether the relationship is going stale because you don't do these simple things anymore or it is because you are smothering her and being too possessive. Over possessiveness is another big cause of relationship failure. When you really care about someone all you want to do is be with them but sometimes it can become too much. If you want to be with her so much that you don't let her go out with her friends or family and you need to know her every move then this can put a big strain on the relationship. If this is the case then you need to back off a little and give her some breathing room.

It can be a little scary and even depressing when the person you love starts to drift away. Don't wait until it's too late before you decide to do anything about it. As soon as you think there may be a problem in your relationship then you need to make some changes to resolve it and make the relationship strong again.

45. How to Get Over Someone You Love - A Heartbreak Guide

Do you know how to get over someone you love? If you have had a deep, meaningful experience with a partner and the relationship goes sour, you may not know how to get over someone you love.

At first, you will feel terribly hurt and alone. Accept your pain – don't fight it. You spent a good amount of time and emotional energy on your ex, and that won't heal in a hurry. It is okay to cry. Talk to your friends and family about how they dealt with a break up.

One useful thing to do at this stage is to write a letter to your ex. Pour out everything that is in your heart. Talk about your love, your expectations, and your pain. Many people find that this letter runs pages in length. Take your time composing it.

Then, when you have said everything that needs saying, roll up the letter and burn it.

That's right. Whatever you do, do not mail this letter to your ex. The purpose of the letter was for you to emote. But, don't keep the

letter lying around either. You want a symbolic ending. Burning gives you a sense of finality that even throwing the letter away won't give you.

As you get a little bit of perspective on the relationship, the next step in how to get over someone you love is to analyze what went wrong. As unlikely as it seems right now, you will have other relationships. If you learn from the mistakes in this one, the next one has a better chance of success.

Keep your distance from your ex. That will help you in how to get over someone you love. As soon after the break up as possible, exchange any property you have of each other, and then do a complete separation for 30 days. Agree that you won't call, text, or email each other for a month. This will give you time to recover from the break up.

Use this time to work on areas of your own life that you have neglected. If you have ignored friends because your romantic relationship took up too much time, use this period in your life to reconnect. Friends can provide a valuable support network during this time.

Start working on your own emotional and physical health during this time. Take time to go to the gym and consider getting therapy to help your psyche heal.

You should also look into ways to improve yourself. Join a hiking club. Take a class at the local community center. Take tango lessons. As you work on becoming a better person, the hurt of the relationship will begin to fade away.

You will meet a whole new circle of people when you get involved in activities you enjoy. Some of these people will become friends. And, one may become a soulmate.

And isn't forming a new relationship the ultimate answer to the question "how to get over someone you love?"

46. Use this System to Succeed with Women

I know it's a jungle out there in the dating world and at times you just feel like giving up on the dating game. Sometimes your fear of failure holds you back and you don't do a damn thing to improve your love life.

If you're in a dating rut, let me suggest some ways to get you back on track and get the love and romance in your life that you deserve:

1. The most important thing you can do is to force yourself to take action and follow through on meeting and approaching women.

2. It's very important to monitor your results and progress. Keep track of what methods you are using to meet new women and notice if they are working or not. I would suggest keeping a journal and putting it in writing.

3. Whatever you do, don't feel sorry for yourself if what you're doing is not working. Don't give up hope and drop out of the dating game.

4. My last suggestion is the most important of all. If what you're doing to meet single women and find romance is not working, try something else.

And if that doesn't work, Don, what do I do? Try something else! You just keep trying until you finally succeed. And trust me guys, if you're persistent and take action, backed with faith and belief, you will succeed with women beyond your wildest dreams. Guaranteed!

47. Tips for Shy Men

The question remains, whether you, as a shy man can develop your own powers of attracting women, your own personal version of the knack. It is a matter of attuning yourself to the burning flame The question remains, whether you, as a shy man can develop your own powers of attracting women, your own personal version of the knack. It is a matter of attuning yourself to the burning flame within you, of recognizing your own specialness, your uniqueness as a human being.

This reaches far beyond issues of confidence and self-esteem, it touches upon your ultimate faith in yourself as a part of the Grand Design. You must affirm your belief that you are capable of forming stable relationships with women, and that this is an essential element in your life's work.

Finally, it comes down to translating purpose and intention into action, of getting to the point that your everyday interactions with women mirror your inner feelings toward them.

If you like women, enjoy their company, and know how to express it in a tactful, understated manner, they will respond. Listen to the women in your life, be sympathetic, give them emotional support,

and you will be amply repaid. You will develop a talent for attracting the women who need what you have to offer - your own unique self, encompassing all of you, your strengths as well as your weaknesses, your luminous humanity as well as your warts. This is your "knack."

48. All About Loving Yourself First To Get Others To Love You Back

When it comes to love, you get what you give. Love yourself first before you can expect others to love you back. Admittedly, your insecurities get in the way at times. You hone in on all your weaknesses instead of taking pride in your strengths. You need to celebrate each day of your life, even if some of the times things get difficult. Life can be trying, but everyone has his or her own burden to carry.

More importantly, know that you're worth so much more. Take pride in who you are and what you have because you've worked hard to achieve so many things in life. You may not succeed in every endeavor, but this doesn't mean that all hope is lost.

It's time to take back what's yours and to look forward to what you can make of your future. You have so much potential in you. As long as you have the strength to get out of bed each day, you can create a future of your dreams of finding someone to love.

Getting Out of the Rut

It's okay to feel depressed every now and then. Yes, you need to sulk some of the time. Cry for all your failures but refuse to let your emotions rule you. Just know that if you had everything handed to you on a silver platter, you'll never get to really appreciate your blessings.

Feelings of satisfaction come when you're able to overcome barriers. It's necessary to know that there are also good times in store and that it's all up to you to change things for the better. After you're done with all the whining, make a promise to yourself to do better. Don't dwell too much on all the pain because you've already done that. Instead, summon the strength to push forward.

Go Out with People Who Appreciate You

Admittedly, you do meet toxic people along the way. Don't let them get to you. They're also dealing with their own issues.

Then, there are the successful ones. Don't measure yourself against them. Rather, see them as your inspiration and recognize your own uniqueness. Success can be defined in so many ways. What works for some may not always work for you.

Focus on what you have and stop comparing yourself to those whom you think are better. Set realistic goals instead because you can achieve more when you're aware of what you're capable of. Take time to enjoy life. Pretty soon, you'll attract partners who'll appreciate you for being you.

The Secret

The ultimate secret to being happy with your relationships is to take time to do the things you love most. Because you'll be surprised at how this simple decision can give you back the energy that's been depleted by all that negativity.

Take a look at everything you have. Every single blessing counts. The little things are just as important as the big things. This is when you start rearranging your priorities.

Work hard at improving every single thing a step at a time. If you need to alter some aspects in your life, go ahead and do it. Just make sure you do all these for you, and not for someone else. The change could actually be refreshing.

Then soon enough, you'll get to see how life starts to unfold. Love is just around the bend, but you will only meet it if you look inside first.

49. Men Dating Taller Women - Success Tips

There are a lot of really tall women out there. And there are a lot of not-so-tall men who are attracted to them. But many feel that men dating taller women is an impossibility. Here are some tips for you shorter guys that can prove this wrong.

1. Don't make it an issue. Maybe you've tried approaching taller women before only to be shunned or laughed at. Maybe you've never even tried it out of fear or intimidation. Here's one thing you need to understand. Most tall women are perfectly fine with the fact that they are tall and you should be too. If you feel intimidated, it's because you are creating that feeling yourself. Most tall women are not going to purposefully try to intimidate anyone. Their height is not something they will use against you. Like any woman, tall women care about what kind of guy you are. Not how tall (or short) you are.

2. Whatever you do. . .do NOT use the cheesy tall-women joke lines. Do you think that tall women have never heard them? That you are the first to show your "witty self?" Do you want to make an impression? Don't even bring up the issue of height in any way, shape or form - hers or yours. Talk about something, anything, else.

3. Sadly, this seems to be one of the harder tasks for men dating taller women. Tall women want to be cuddled too. Hold their hand, put your arms around them. Wine and dine them. Maybe because of their height, they appear too strong to need this kind of attention. But they do. Show them that you love them for their height without making an issue out of it.

4. Ditch the sexual anxiety that you won't measure up in the bedroom. When it comes to sex, everyone is the same height.

5. This is a pretty obvious one but it's easy to do and makes a difference. Stop slouching and always practice good posture. Standing up straight not only makes you look taller, it actually makes you act and feel more confident. Always stand up straight with your shoulders squared. Make the most of your physical frame.

6. When in doubt, look at the stars. All of these famous on-the-short-side guys are dating (or married to) taller women: Michael J. Fox, Martin Sheen, Al Pacino, Tom Cruise, Emilio Estevez, Dustin Hoffman, and Prince, just to name a few.

7. Stop worrying about what other people think. If you happen to be one of those men dating taller women, do you know what other guys are thinking when they see the two of you together? They're thinking. . ."he must be filthy rich" or they are thinking. . ." he must be great in the sack". Not bad, huh?

50. 5 Lessons From Previous Break Ups

While a lot of guys may not be so quick to admit it, I have been dumped by a lot of women over the years. Perhaps you have, too; maybe not. Either way, I'm a firm believer in learning from the mistakes of other people. With that in mind, I'd like to share some things that I have learned from the women who have dumped me, in the hopes that it will help your relationship go more smoothly.

Lesson #1: Share and share alike. What this means is that each person is likely to blame the other for the break up. But the truth is that you both contributed to the break up in some way. By taking an honest look at what went wrong, and your role in it, you can make a conscious effort to avoid making the same mistakes in the future.

Lesson #2: Women still need their space. As a guy it may seem that women always like to snuggle and cuddle and that they are always around. But they still need some time alone. To make things worse, a lot of guys can be possessive and try to know what their partner is up to at all times. And if you have had a woman that was unfaithful in the past, then this tendency is even stronger. While that may be the case, by doing this you are showing distrust, and no relationship can survive in that kind of atmosphere. So, even though it can be hard, do your best to let your girlfriend do the things she likes to do, and don't feel that you always have to give her the third degree about what she's doing.

Lesson #3: Time heals. The first few days after a break up are the absolute worst. After that, you will start to come to terms with what happened. Sure, there will be emotional ups and downs, but it will get easier as time goes on. If it doesn't, then it may be a good idea to see a qualified counselor to help you. You can also use this pain in the future by reminding yourself it's easier to work on the tough problems while you are in the relationship than it is to suffer through a break up.

Lesson

Lesson #4: Accept the facts. When first starting a relationship, you may feel as though you have found your soulmate. You were even imagining a wonderful future together, and may have even talked about it. But, over time, things start to go downhill. You start to wonder what you ever saw in her, and she probably feels the same way about you. Then you break up. Now you don't just feel bad about splitting up, you also feel bad about missing out on the future you imagined. However, remember that it's better to end things now if it really wasn't meant to be.

Lesson #5: Happiness isn't an accident. To put it another way: Relationships take work. You can't just let stuff happen to you, you have to take responsibility for making it what you want it to be. This may be the most important lesson of all.

How to Date Young Women

51. Younger Women Dating Older Men - Biological Destiny?

Younger women dating older men has been common throughout the centuries. This is, in large part, due to biology. Women in their child bearing years look to older, more financially secure men to provide for their children. Men look for fertile women to pass along their genes. But, is there more to this younger women dating older men scenario?

Biology is not destiny. There are many instances of older women dating younger men. Take Demi Moore and Ashton Kutcher for instance. But, on the whole, you will usually find younger women dating older men.

Even though birth rates have plunged and many men forgo having children altogether, the idea of dating a younger woman hasn't gone away. In fact, having a sexy girlfriend or wife may be more important if children are not a factor in the relationship.

Similarly, even though many women are capable of financially supporting their children without a man's help, the idea of dating older men is still prevalent. Though women can even have children through artificial insemination or adoption with no man involved, younger women dating older men is still strong.

Part of the appeal for men is that they want glamorous, sexy, young looking trophies to show off to their friends. Just as they want the best cars, watches, boats, and airplanes, they want the woman they are dating to be a status symbol.

For younger women, dating an older man may also be a status symbol. A woman who can attract an older, wealthy man may feel more secure about her sexual appeal.

In many cases, when an older man dates a younger woman, he has been married previously. He might have children from that relationship that the new girlfriend has to cope with. He might also not have as much money as it appears at first because he may be providing financial support to those children and an ex wife.

Because he's been burned before, women in these relationships have to understand the realities of dating an older man. For instance, he may ask for a prenuptial agreement before marriage. This doesn't mean he thinks a marriage will fail, but if it does, he wants to protect himself.

In general, older men will look for good looks in the younger women they are dating. She will have charm, education, and social skills to help him advance in his career.

Younger women often pick up their dates at charity events and fundraisers, high end hotel bars, expensive restaurants, exclusive country clubs, and at gatherings for high end hobbies such as boating shows. Older men know that the single women gathered at such places are often on the lookout for them.

Younger women dating older men is a phenomenon that has gone

back to the days when the Biblical commandment "go forth and multiply" was a priority for the species. But even though the planet is overpopulated, some biological facts don't change. That is why younger women dating older men is still a main factor in society today.

52. Dating Young Women – A Guide for Older Guys

Dating young women is a particular challenge for guys. If you are dating women who are under the age of 25 and you are 7 or more years older than she is, you need to read this article on dating young women.

There is a stereotype that women who date older men are gold diggers. But, this applies to very few women. Actually, many young women are just out to have a good time. They are not looking for marriage. If you happen to be attracted to a younger woman, you need to play into this "good time image."

Younger women are more whimsical, flirty, passionate, and romantic than their older sisters. They're less ready to settle down and have children. You will get a lot of mileage out of having a youthful outlook. Being recklessly spontaneous, maintaining a high level of energy, and focusing on the emotional connections will go a long way to helping you with dating young women.

To this end, you can't be emotionally needy when dating young women. For instance, if you were dating a woman near your own age, you would pick up the phone every time she called. You might return her text within 5 minutes. A younger woman doesn't need this kind of intensity. You can wait to return a text or let a call go to voicemail.

Many men who are dating young women are conscious of the age difference and are insecure about being older. This will actually hasten the break up. Don't bring up the issue of age unless she does. Also, don't make cracks about her youth or about "cradle snatching." Don't refer to yourself as her "daddy." When you are unfazed about the age difference, she will be too.

As an older man, you have several advantages over the frat boy guys she is used to dating.

You have more experience. You are interested in things beyond the latest video game release. You make more money and can take her to more upscale places.

You are also more sexually sophisticated. You will know how to satisfy her in bed and be more in tune with her needs.

Men mature more slowly than women, which may be why so many young women look to date older men. They are looking for someone in their same range of emotional development.

Dating young women isn't just a modern thing either. In every society across all time, there has been a gap in the average age of coupling men and women. While in the United States right now, that gap is a mere 2 years, in many societies that gap ranges from an average of 5 to 15 years.

If you are interested in dating young women, be aware that there are challenges posed because of societal expectations and conditioning. However, there are many advantages to dating young women.

53. Why Are Older Men Dating Younger Women

Older men dating younger women are becoming a more popular phenomenon, especially in recent years. When an older significant other is with a younger one, this is commonly referred to as a May

December romance, because there is a significant age difference between the woman and the man, or the man and the woman. While it appears much more common for younger men to date older women, older men dating younger women is also becoming a popular phenomenon, even though some will view it to be out of place.

Generally speaking, in situations of older men dating younger women, the younger woman is generally looking for something specific. It is a known fact that women can be attracted to older men for a number of reasons. This does not necessarily mean that an early twenties woman will date a man of seventy five, but rather relative to their age, women are more than willing to date men who are a few years older than them, and this is how older men dating younger women comes into play.

In many cases, women are looking for their husband to be. The qualities that women are looking for in their future husbands are the same qualities that men slightly older than them are displaying. Most women are more than willing to admit that they are looking for a strong and confident man. Women are not necessarily looking for young and virile hunter gatherer types, but when it comes to older men dating younger women, the qualities that shine through usually begin with a man's ability to support a family, or provide for that family on a long term basis. So usually in situations with older men dating younger women, the woman is looking for a man she can settle down with, regardless of whether or not this is what the man is looking for.

The traits that women are looking for in "husband material" are most commonly found in men aged eighteen and older, and as women age, they are still consistently looking for someone older, because it is assumed that older men are more civilized, more mature and more capable of providing for whoever they are with. This is the reason why older men dating younger women is becoming commonplace today. Women are constantly on the lookout for someone older and more mature, and most men seem to have no problem providing most of what these women are looking for, as they get to date younger as a result.

In these situations of older men dating younger women, the men are looking for something completely different, because most do not select younger women as ideal wife material. Still, in these

situations, both the man and the woman in the relationship seem to get the traits and characteristics that they need, and if the relationship works and everyone is satisfied, that's really all there is.

54. Things To Know Before You Start Dating Young Women

Are you considering dating young women? What are the things you should consider before going out with a woman who is younger than you? Are there advantages and disadvantages? Here are seven rules for dating young women.

1. Accept when dating younger women that she is from a different "generation" than you. Even if she is only ten years younger than you, her life experiences have been different. The music she listened to as a teenager, the television shows and movies she likes, and even her political worldview have been shaped by different experiences. Her vocabulary may be slightly different (like, she says "like" a lot). The further apart in age you are, the more pronounced these differences will be.

2. Accept that she has fewer life experiences than you do. If she's in her early 20's and you are in your 40's, she's just beginning to experience adult life. She may want to go out partying while you want a night in or a sophisticated evening. While her electric personality may attract you at first, working out a compromise between her need to go out and your need to stay in will keep you in the relationship for the long haul.

3. Accept that, in part, your attractiveness to her is based on the idea that you have financial security. You may feel like you have no money because of debt, alimony, or child support obligations, but she will see that paycheck of yours as "big money" compared to her own entry level salary. She will expect you to provide nice things and experiences for her. Expect to pick up the check when dating younger women.

4. She will find your maturity and wisdom sexy. One of the things she likes about you is that you're not an overgrown teenager. Don't try to act like you are 20. There are plenty of 20 year old men that she could go out with. She chose you precisely because you're not one of those guys.

5. You can't be needy. While it is not good to be needy with a woman of any age, younger women are not likely to put up with your clinginess. She is going to be wary of why you are not already with a woman your own age, so she'll be on guard for any sign that you might need her more than she needs you. When she texts or phones you, don't feel that you have to respond right away. By putting her on a short leash, you will actually be able to keep her longer.

6. Don't be insecure. Similar to the advice above, you shouldn't feel that she has "graced" you with her presence. Sure, she's hot. But, you have a lot of qualities that make you attractive too. That's why she's going out with you. Don't be insecure about your relationship when dating young women. It just puts them off.

7. Be mature. She is attracted to a man who is a few years older than herself because she is looking for someone who is stable and more experienced. Don't try to act her age. Be a man of your own age. Your maturity is a natural draw for her.

And, there you have it. A real man's guide to dating young women.

55. First Date Tips

There are many right and wrong things to do when you go on a date. Knowing what you should be focusing on and what you need to avoid on a first date can mean the difference between a second date and having someone that never calls you again. If you know what makes a perfect date, you can then go into a first date with confidence and self assurance. You will know what you are doing and what to expect. This limits the surprises that sometimes come up and can ruin a date.

1. Be On Time:

One very important thing that you should do when you are going on a first date is to make sure that you are on time. The fastest way to make a bad impression is to show up late. If you are late, your date will think that you do not care about them or that they are not important enough for you to be on time.

Another potential result is that your date may decide that they do not want to wait for you and will leave before you arrive. They say that the first impression is the lasting impression. Being on time for a date makes a great impression.

2. Put Your Date at Ease:

Do your best to make your date feel as comfortable as possible. Everyone gets very nervous when they go on a first date with someone. If you are making your date feel comfortable, you will also find that you are more relaxed and enjoy yourself much more during the date. Laughing at your date's jokes is one great way to make them feel that you are interested in them and it will also make them more comfortable.

3. Keep Conversation Alive:

Be interesting and keep the conversation alive. You do not want to show up for a date and then have nothing to say and nothing to ask all night. You should prepare yourself ahead of time and think of interesting topics and things that make good conversation.

4. Listen Sincerely:

Show a valid interest in what your date has to say. Pay attention when they are talking to you. Let them know that you care what they are saying. Practice your conversation skills ahead of time. This will help you prepare for the date.

5. Don't Talk About Yourself:

You do not want to talk about yourself all night. This is a turn off and is also rude. You do not want to come off as being conceited or stuck on yourself. Ask questions about your date. Give them a chance to talk. It is not all about you. If you do all the talking and do not let them get a word in, chances are it will be your only date with them.

6. No Talking About Past Relationships:

Do not talk about your past relationships. No one really wants to hear about your ex. They do not want to know what the good points and bad points are. This is a huge turn off and a guaranteed way to drastically reduce the chances for a second date. This is a new person and a new start. Focus on the date that you are with and start finding out about them.

56. Romantic Tips to Use on Women

Give her a morning treat. No, not that kind of treat. Wake up early and fix her cup of coffee. Think small but thoughtful. Romance is in the details. Does she prefer tea with lemon or a boiled egg with a sliced apple? Whatever it is, show her you know her every desire with a simple piece of toast.

Create a private moment. There is always time for romance. Keep a CD of her favorite love songs in the car. Pop it into the CD player during an everyday drive and instantly create a romantic moment. Intimate and personal, she will feel like every love song was written for her.

Feed her cravings. Chocolate is a romantic gesture, but personalization is more important than tradition. Go across town and pick up the favorite red velvet cupcake she only buys on special occasions. Or pick up her favorite candy bar or French fries. Not only are you presenting her with a guilty pleasure, giving food unconsciously represents you love her no matter her appearance.

Text your love. The text message is the new version of the love letter. Done properly it is just as romantic. Send a text message that is a touching reminder she is being remembered during the day. It can be as simple as "I'm thinking of you and want to let you know I love you," or "Waiting for you at home, come back soon. I miss you." You can step it up a notch with a text series. Early in the day text "Why I love you." Then send multiple emails throughout the day describing in detail why you love them. For example, "You've seen me at my best and my worst, yet love me anyway," or "You make me feel cherished." Pour out your heart and you can't go wrong.

57. Advice for Average Guys Dating Beautiful Women

Have you asked a beautiful woman out on a date and are still in shock that she accepted? Men often put beautiful women on a pedestal which can make it a challenge for an 'average' guy to date one.

Dating beautiful women can really boost the ego of a man. He will be beaming with pride when he walks down the street with this beautiful woman by his side. Not only does he get an ego boost but he will also look pretty impressive to other guys. Dating a beautiful woman will also make the guy more desirable to other women.

An attractive woman can probably date any man she likes, even rich, powerful men. Because they are so appealing to men for their beauty they often develop some back habits that may make them less desirable as a long term partner. Many beautiful women are vain, manipulative and high maintenance.

If you aren't very wealthy and you are fairly average looking then it can be very challenging to date a beautiful woman. Here is some advice for dating beautiful women.

1. Stand out from the crowd. Beautiful women have men fawning over them all the time and they probably all look the same to her, so to get her attention you need to be different from the rest.

2. Don't treat her like a goddess - every other man is doing this so this is just average to her. You can differentiate yourself by not treating her like she is a goddess but act indifferent to her as though you aren't even attracted to her looks. It is the guys that appear not to be interested that she will want - this goes along the lines of people always wanting what they can't have. By ignoring her you are giving her a challenge that she will respond to.

3. Pay more attention to her 'plain Jane' friend. A beautiful woman won't understand why you would prefer her plain friend over her and she will get quite jealous. She won't want her friend getting all the attention and she will begin to flirt with you to win over your attention.

4. Instead of giving her compliments, tease her. Most other men will shower her with compliments, which she probably expects and is probably quite mundane to her now. If you light-heartedly tease her about any flaws then this is a different approach from what she is used to and she will respond well to that.

5. Don't just look at her outer beauty but also focus on her inner beauty. Don't spend all night staring at her like she is a goddess but instead show that you are interested in her as a person. Ask her questions about her life, her interests and hobbies. She will respond well to a man that she knows is interested in her as a person and not just for her beauty.

6. Don't call her too soon. Most men will probably call her the next day and she may even expect that. Wait a couple of days before calling her and she will respect you for it because you have impressed her so far with the above tips and now you are showing her even more that you are not desperate and just after her for her beauty.

7. Don't try to get her into bed on the first date. Of course you are sexually attracted to her and most likely all men she dates try to get her into bed straight away. By playing a little hard to get will spike

her interest in you and also reinforce the fact that you like her as a person and not just a sex object.

You should remember that beauty is only skin deep and although it is great to date beautiful women, ultimately you also want a woman who is beautiful on the inside too. Take the time to get to know this woman and you may have found yourself a beautiful woman inside and out.

58. Coworker Relationships

A relationship that develops between coworkers is often frowned upon very highly. There are some businesses and organizations that strictly forbid interoffice relationships.

There is really no conscious control over who we fall in love with. It is not something that we have complete control and power over. There is certain chemistry within our bodies and signals that are given off by our brains. It is something that is subconsciously occurring and out of our control.

So, no matter how many times you read your company handbook and find that you are not supposed to have a relationship with anyone at work, if you are truly attracted to someone that you work with, you are not going to be able to fight that attraction.

So, what do you do if you find that you want to date a coworker? First of all, you have to make a decision between the two of you. Talk with the coworker. Chances are they have given off some sort of signal or vibe that has made you take notice of them. This is more than likely a mutual attraction. It is possible to make a relationship with a coworker work well for both of you. It is also possible in some circumstances to maintain this relationship without reprimand or repercussions. You just have to be smart and sensible about what you are doing.

If you find yourself starting a relationship with a coworker, the worst thing that you can do is try to hide it. This will have serious consequences in the end when people find out about it, which they always do. Be open and honest. Talk with your boss about what is going on. In most cases, if you go to them and you are completely honest, there are ways that they can make it work for you. However, if you hide the relationship and your boss finds out later, you could find yourself out of a job and in a bad situation.

You should also talk openly with your partner. Make sure that you both understand that your relationship does not affect your work. You cannot play favorites or change the way that you work because of this new relationship. Keep in mind that at work, everything is to remain the same.

If your partner is higher up than you and is required to reprimand you for something that you have done wrong relating to work, they need to be able to do that without bias. If your relationship starts interfering with your work, you need to take a serious look at everything that is involved and find out where you can make changes.

In some cases, one party in a relationship will choose to leave their job. This is often a personal decision and not one that they are forced into by their employer. They do not want to have a relationship with someone that they work with everyday. If the relationship is that important to them, they may very well be willing to find a new job to maintain that relationship and make it as good as they possibly can.

59. Alpha Males

Alpha is the first letter of the Greek alphabet. In astronomy, it is the brightest star in a constellation. In common parlance, alpha means to be the first.

Alpha males are guys who seem to be leading the pack, the hunter, the ever-reliable male god. They are all around us, in the ranks burly blue collar workers to the impeccable corporate leaders.

So why do women like alpha males; or do they?

Women do not only like alpha males; they adore them! Alpha males are the stuff that women's romantic imaginations are of. These are men who get women's attention wherever they go.

The attraction lies in the power seemingly possessed by alpha males. It's not really just about the money but it is about strength in character and the ability to be respected by his peers.

A woman defines an alpha male as someone who is vocal about what he wants and who does everything to get it. An alpha male is not just cocky out loud, but there is a semblance of authority in his voice that seems to attract others, male or female. An alpha male is filled with confidence about his looks though he may not be handsome and is confident about his intelligence though he may not be a Wharton College graduate.

In the animal kingdom the alpha males are those who lead the pack with aggressive behavior. The animals have their own social structure where the alpha or the dominant males get to mate with the females, with the principle that the alpha males will most probably produce better offspring. Same goes for the alpha males in the society of humans.

Women describe alpha males as those with an innate superiority and who literally leads the pack. These are males who are aggressive and assertive despite their limitations.

To be able to understand an alpha male, one has to get to know his characteristics such as but not limited to being:

Born leaders

Alpha males are born to lead the pack. They are known to be the peacemakers and the ones responsible for stopping fights after and aggression usually started off by a bully. These men are usually dignified men who have leadership capabilities and they sometimes rule their world. An alpha male is a no nonsense leader who cannot be dictated upon and who stands by his principles.

Gandhi is an alpha male. He is a charismatic leader who refused to be pressured into giving up his cause. He was able to win his battle by espousing non-violence. Microsoft czar Bill Gates is an example of an alpha male who continues to change the world and its people. There are many alpha males in a variety of settings, all of whom have provided inspiration and great leadership to their sectors. Most alpha males are attracted and married to strong and outstanding women.

Confident

Alpha males are so sure of themselves but not to the point of being cocky. They have high self esteem, believing that they have the power to do anything they want and to achieve their dreams. They know they have that special something within them but they do not boast nor talk about their strength.

Women are attracted to the alpha because of the confidence that emanates from them. This confidence manifests itself in the way he carries himself and the way he deals with others. This confidence is shown in the way he does things and treats other people. The alpha male's high self esteem makes him confident that he can get the best girl in town. The truth is, the girls usually flock around him.

Assertive

Being confident of himself and in what he can achieve, the alpha male is always assertive but not to the point of being pushy. He knows what he wants and how to get it. He asserts his rights and the rights of his friends. This may be the reason why alpha males are so popular with the pack. He leads them and gives them protection. Women love the alpha male for being assertive, of being able to know he can do it and doing something to achieve what he wants to do.

Born leaders, confident and assertive. These are the qualities that make women swoon over the alpha male. Need we say more?

60. Perfect Relationships... Do They Exist

People say that the only perfect relationships that exist are those between a blind woman and a deaf man. He can't hear her nagging and she can't see all the mess he creates on those odd occasions when he tries to complete one simple domestic chore.

Seriously, what do you need for a great partnership? If you ask any old couple who have been together for decades, they will tell you honesty, respect, trust and a healthy dose of sexual attraction. The lust does wear off after the first heady couple of years but it should be replaced by a mutual fascination strong enough to ward off all temptation.

Honesty is important between couples. Even simple things such as always doing what you say will pay off huge dividends.

No relationship is without its ups and downs, but if you know your partner always means what he says, it helps to trust him when things do get tough.

Trust doesn't just mean that you feel secure when he is with other women. It also means that you know he will be there for you. That he believes in you and your abilities as a person, a mother or whatever role you fill in life. And it goes both ways, you have to believe in him too.

Mutual respect is also very important. Life is difficult and there are enough people out there who will put you down without your partner doing it too. If you do have disagreements, keep it private. It is pointless and disrespectful to share the intimate details of your sorrow with the whole world. When you have forgotten about it someone else is bound to remember and remind you!

Sometimes things can get a little stale in the bedroom. Life gets in the way either through having kids or stressful jobs, or financial problems. While you will not be making love as often as you did when you first met, if it has been a while you need to address it. There is a secret bond that keeps couples together and that only comes about by being intimate. It is not all about sex though. Gentle touching, a lingering hug, just holding hands and a whispered "I love you" are just as important, if not more important.

To have a deeply loving relationship you need to trust the other person with your heart. You must be able to tell them your innermost secrets and desires. Sharing special moments will help to deepen the bond that exists between you.

It is often difficult to remember to put your relationship as a priority but unless you nurture it, it may fade and die. Yes it may take some juggling but try and arrange a night just for the two of you to enjoy. Ban all talk of your relatives, the kids, your finances and aim to concentrate on each other. It doesn't need to end up in the bedroom; well not always!

Sharing good times will help you through the dark days that hit every couple, even those in perfect relationships.

61. How to Ask Women for a Date

There are good ways and bad ways to ask a girl out. The bad way to ask a girl out is, "Would you like to go out with me?" By saying this:

- You set yourself up for rejection. She might say no.

- You imply that she would be doing you a favor by going out with you.
- You imply a formal date. You are making a move on her. The pressure is on her.
- If she says "no," you are never sure whether to ask her again for another time. Was it, "No, I don't want to go out with you," or "No, I want to go out with you but I'm busy that night."
- You literally sound like a junior high kid asking a girl out on his first date.

The right way to ask a single girl out is, "Let's get together and do something sometime." Memorize these words. By saying this, you give an impression of a casual meeting. No big deal.

Friends getting to know each other. Not a formal date. If you say this, her response will let you know whether she wants to date you or not.

If she is interested, she will respond in the positive, but also her tone will be positive. The expression on her face will be positive. She may even lead the conversation to making a specific time to do something. If you do get a positive response, you can either pursue the conversation and arrange to meet on a casual date or leave it until the next time you meet. You know she wants to get together and she will be waiting, now that you have teased her with talk of a date but offered no specific plans. You are being elusive and playing hard to get. Her anticipation works in your favor.

If she does not want to go out with you, her verbal response may be "no" or it may even be "yes" to save your feelings, but her tone, her facial expression, and her desire to drop the subject will let you know she is not interested. Don't pursue it further.

The beauty of this exact phrase is:

- You are not set up for rejection. After all, you have not really asked her out. You've made a statement.

- You are throwing out an offer. The implication is that you are doing her a favor. She is not doing you a favor by going out with you.
- It implies a casual get-together to get to know each other, not a formal date.
- You know for sure whether she wants to date you or not.
- You aren't asking her. You are making a statement which says something about you. You are the type of person that likes to do things with friends, and of course she would like to participate. After all, there is no pressure. You are a confident, friendly, fun-loving person who is doing things.

Now re-read that phrase. "Let's get together and do something sometime." See how much better it is than asking a question that may get you a wrong answer?

62. Facing the Challenge of College Dating

Students facing the transition from high school to college are likely facing the biggest challenge they've ever had to face. Expectations are raised, both for themselves and from others. Moving on to college means moving on to a new level of academic performance. It's the time when most of us move beyond being a not so serious teenager to a very serious adult who is focused on furthering their education and planning for their future. Not only are we expected to think more seriously about ourselves, but at the same time many of us find that we're leaving behind some of the relationships we've formed throughout our earlier school years. Best friends, acquaintances, team members, and even boyfriends and girlfriends are sometimes left behind as we move onto the next important stage in our lives and maturity.

So how difficult is it to handle this serious emotional, physical, academic, and personal change? College life can be intimidating, particularly for those who decide to attend school away from home. Moving away means not only losing the relationships they've grown comfortable with for so many years, but in many cases losing the emotional support system their family has been for them through their younger years. All aspects of college life may be completely foreign to the new college student, and college dating only complicates matters. Why? Because at times many outgoing and engaging young people who had no problem creating dating relationships in high school may be intimidated by the prospect of dating a new "class" of potential partner.

The thing to remember about college dating is that one shouldn't approach it as such a serious process. There is plenty of "serious" stuff going on in your transition from high school teen to college adult, so to put too much emphasis on being serious about a

relationship is not what college dating should be about. Try and approach college dating as a way to share the college experience with someone who shares similar interests and preferences. Seek out dating relationships with classmates who are studying the same classes or are on the same degree track. In this way, you can be sure that your comfort level is established prior to beginning the formal dating process.

College dating doesn't have to be difficult. A new college student already faces enough of a challenge in this very important stage in their lives, so being too serious about their approach to dating shouldn't overwhelm them. There's plenty of time to be serious about a partner, but if a casual college dating relationship grows on its own into something more substantial, then at least it will come as a result of a natural process rather than an unnecessary focus on being overly serious.

63. 10 Incredibly Nice Things to Do For Her

You can demonstrate your love for the special woman in your life in a number of small ways. Flowers and candy on special occasions are always nice but you can also surprise a woman by offering smaller gestures on a daily basis. She will appreciate your thoughtfulness and understand that you are trying to show her how much she means to you.

One incredibly nice thing to do for her is simply to ask her how her day was and listen intently to her answer. Women enjoy talking about their personal issues and expressing an interest in her career or other areas of interest will be greatly appreciated. Listening carefully to her will let her know that you are interested in her thoughts and care about her feelings.

Cooking for a woman is another incredibly nice thing that you can do for her. Most women are the primary cooks in the relationship and giving her a night off from her usual kitchen duties is always a welcomed gesture. Don't worry if you don't know how to cook, it's really not that hard. There are many cook books and Internet sites that offer a wide variety of recipes. Pick one that sounds interesting and follow the instructions carefully.

Remembering and celebrating a small occasion is another nice gesture that women appreciate. It's always nice to celebrate on big occasions but if you remember the anniversary of another special day the woman in your life will be completely caught by surprise. For example, celebrate the anniversary of the day you brought home your new puppy with a trip to a dog park.

Another incredibly nice thing to do for a woman is to give her compliments when they are unexpected. Women expect compliments when they put a lot of effort into their appearance but letting her know you think she is beautiful while she's running errands, demonstrates that you see her inner beauty shining through at all times. Compliments don't always have to be about physical characteristics either. You could compliment her on her career accomplishments and let her know that you appreciate how hard she works.

Handing over the remote control is another incredibly nice thing you can do for a woman. You may not want to sit through another episode of a home decorating show but allowing the woman in your life to indulge in this without complaining about her choice will show her that you are not belittling her interests.

If you want to do something really nice for the special woman in your life, get to know her family and friends. Women value their relationships and she will be pleased about the fact that you take an interest in and get to know the other special people in her life. Caring about those that she loves shows her that you love her.

Still another incredibly nice thing to do for a woman is to write her a love letter and send it in the mail. Sure she sees you every day and you may even exchange emails and phone calls on a daily basis but a love letter is something that she can save in a special place and will cherish. Expressing your love in a letter is a special way to tell a woman that you care deeply about her.

Planning a trip for your woman is another incredibly nice thing you can do for her. A vacation is always nice but when you take the initiative and plan out all the details ahead of time, it shows that you want her to have the enjoyable experience of the trip but that you are willing to take care of all the planning. Women tend to take the lead in making travel arrangements and verifying the logistics of trips but if you take care of that ahead of time, the woman is free to just focus on packing for the trip.

Another incredibly nice thing to do for a woman is to surprise her at work by showing up for a lunch date. Women always love to be surprised and your lunch date will give her the opportunity to get out of the office for a little while and enjoy some time with you. Many women skip lunch or work straight through it but giving her the opportunity to break away from her desk for even a half hour will give her a welcomed chance to relax a little bit.

Finally if you want to do something really nice for the woman in your life, it could be as simple as opening the car door for her when you go out. Women enjoy being independent but small chivalrous gestures are always appreciated. If you normally rush to the driver's side of the car and hop in, stop once in a while to open her door first. It will show her that you want to protect and care for her and will make her feel well loved.

There are many ways you can show your love for the special woman in your life. Many of the items listed above may be seemingly small, inconsequential things but it is these little things that really show a woman that you care. Doing nice things for a woman demonstrates that you want to go out of your way to make sure that she is happy.

How to Date Cougars

64. Hot And Sexy Mature Women Dating Younger Guys

Mature women dating younger guys is a trend that has just started to pick up steam, but it is not going away any time soon. In fact, more than a quarter of today's brides are older than their grooms.

Celebrity culture has played into this in part. Many well known actresses such as Demi Moore, Madonna, and Susan Sarandon have married younger men. These women have put their stamp of approval on the mature women dating younger men concept.

But, society has changed as well. Not too long ago, women married young and marriages were for life. The nuclear family unit was the basis for society and anything that deviated from this norm was shunned. Therefore, there weren't many opportunities for mature women dating younger men.

But, since divorce has become more prevalent, there are many women in their late 30s and 40s who are looking for partners. When they look at men their own age, they often don't like what they see.

First of all, men who are in this age range are caught up in their own careers and interests. They are less likely to be supportive of a woman's career. Because women have moved into managerial and entrepreneurial roles, they sometimes need partners who can be "the man behind the woman." Men their own age are reluctant to take on this role.

Also, mature women dating men their own age are likely to be disappointed in the sex. A woman peaks sexually in her late 30s. Well into her 40s, she is in her sexual prime. A man, however, begins to lose steam at this age. He's just not able to keep up with her surging needs.

Younger men find these women, newly confident in their sexual prowess, to be very attractive. Mature women know what they want in bed and can communicate that to their lovers.

Mature women dating younger men can also provide the guys with a sense of financial stability that allows the men to take risks with their careers. One younger man was able to pursue a career as a concert pianist because his older woman lover was able to cover their living expenses while he became known in his field. Other men have been able to pursue graduate school or start businesses due to the financial support of their older girlfriends.

Women have, for years, benefited from the generosity of older partners. Now, men are able to do so as well.

If you want to meet a person outside your own age range, you have to go where they are. For instance, a mature woman wanting to date a younger man may want to join a gym. A younger man looking for a professional woman might join a tango class. There are also places for such couples to meet online. The term for this is cougar dating.

Expect that the trend of mature women dating younger men to grow as society's expectations about sex roles evolve.

65. Sexy Older Women Dating Younger Men - Cougars Abound

There is a current trend of older women dating younger men. The popular term for such women is "cougars." Celebrity women who have reached a certain age are finding happiness with younger guys. Demi Moore is perhaps the leading example of this trend as she married Ashton Kutcher who was 15 years her junior. Madonna was married to Guy Richie (10 years younger) and when she split with him, she hooked up with Alex Rodriguez (15 years younger.)

Older women find younger men appealing for several reasons. Cougars tend to be successful career women. They have high level executive positions in major firms or own their own businesses. Many men their own age are threatened by their successes. Younger men, who were raised in a more egalitarian era, are likely to be supportive of the women in their lives.

Older women dating younger men also point to their partner's youthful outlook on life. These men aren't jaded about things like their older counterparts are.

Then there is the sex. Women peak sexually in their late 30s and into their 40s while men reach their greatest performance levels at age 19 and then decline. Many women feel that they missed out on something when they were younger and more inexperienced. The sexual prowess of a younger man is quite attractive to many women in their 30s and 40s.

But, the older women dating younger men trend works both ways. Many younger men find dating an older woman to be very rewarding.

Part of the attraction is certainly sexual. A mature woman knows her body. She knows what pleases her and she is not afraid to take the lead in the bedroom. Guys find this confidence to be quite the turn on.

Young men who date financially secure older women are also more likely to be able to chart their own path in terms of a career. There is less pressure to make money now when a woman can foot some of the bills. Many men dating cougars have found that they can return to graduate school or start a business – risks that wouldn't be possible if they were dating women their own age.

Men are also likely to appreciate that older women are more emotionally mature and less needy. There is quite a bit less drama in an older woman dating younger men. After a fight, an older woman is less likely to call her sister or her best friend to rehash the experience. She'll likely go to bed and tell her boyfriend they can discuss it in the morning.

One of the challenges in these cougar relationships is over fertility. An older woman usually either already has children or doesn't want them. Many of these relationships break up because the man

wants the chance to be a father. If you can weather that storm, the relationships tend to be unusually strong.

Because of societal trends, the older women dating younger men movement is not likely to go away any time soon.

66. A Man's Astrological Guide to Single Women

ARIES (March 21 - April 19) - She's aggressive with men, dynamic, hot-tempered, and very bossy. You must be very strong-willed with this woman and don't let her boss you around. Don't be a wimp, this woman loves a challenge.

She attracts men quite easily and can discard them just as easily. Don't try to tie this woman down, she likes her freedom and doesn't like to be smothered. They are very energetic and aggressive in bed and reach orgasm very quickly. If you want some "hot" romance, this is the girl for you.

TAURUS (April 20 - May 20) - They don't call this the sign of the bull for nothing! This woman is bull-headed and she likes to get her own way and can be very stubborn.

She's very down-to-earth and loves to take care of her man, so be sure and go along with letting her mother you. Shower her with plants, flowers, and money. This woman is very sensual in bed and likes to make love slowly. She can literally make love for hours! I hope you have a lot of sexual stamina to keep up with her!

GEMINI (May 21 - June 21) - This woman is a big flirt, so if you're the jealous and possessive type this can cause problems. She's very intelligent and the best way to her heart is through her mind. You must keep her mind stimulated to keep her from getting bored with you.

She loves to travel, so take her for weekend get-aways out-of-town. She loves to be stroked, so be sure and give her a sensual massage. They love variety in their sex life, so be sure and try

different positions and make love in different settings (in front of the fireplace, in the bathtub or shower, on the kitchen counter, in an open field, etc.).

CANCER (June 22 - July 22) - This woman will want to baby and take care of you. Let her do it, by all means, because it's part of her maternal instincts.

She's very emotional and romantic, so you can really capture this woman's heart by doing anything romantic. She soaks up compliments like a sponge, so be sure to compliment her often. She makes a good sex partner because she will do anything to please her man.

LEO (July 23 - August 22) - This woman is very charming, has lots of sex appeal, and loves to party. She's a very social person and loves to be on the go. If you're a couch potato, you're not the man for her.

Very passionate and affectionate and has lots of love to give to the right guy. Attracted to unusual, dynamic men who are often a bit eccentric. You must be well-dressed and treat her like royalty because she has a strong ego. She's a real tiger in bed and rules the bedroom.

VIRGO (August 23 - September 22) - Very intellectual and a bit cool and acts aloof. Very picky about men and you must meet her high standards. Very critical nature.

Take it slow with this woman. It takes her awhile to warm up to you because of her cautious nature. It's worth it in the end because once she's yours she's yours to keep. Very faithful and devoted. Can be very exacting in bed and wants to follow a set routine. She wants everything to be perfect.

LIBRA (September 23 - October 23) - This is one of the most beautiful signs in the Zodiac. She's very feminine and her good looks attract a lot of men.

She makes an ideal mate because she's so giving and loves peace and harmony. She's so sexy, seductive, and charming. A very social creature and very romantic and sentimental. Be sure and appeal to her romantic nature and she's all yours!

SCORPIO (October 24 - November 21) - This is a very intense and mysterious woman. She doesn't do anything half-hearted and when she sets her sights on a man she will pursue him with relentless intensity. She may even scare you away with her intensity, jealousy, and possessiveness.

She can be a very moody and emotional person. Don't get on the wrong side of this woman because she can make a dangerous enemy and will stop at nothing to get even with you. Very intense in bed and probably the best lover in the Zodiac.

SAGITTARIUS (November 22 - December 21) - She's very independent and loves her freedom. If you try to pin her down and you're the jealous and possessive type, you will scare this woman away.

She loves the outdoors and sports, so plan your activities outside and play sports and attend sporting events. She loves to travel, so take her places to capture her heart. Enjoy her while she's around because her heart is known to wander. She doesn't like long-term commitments. You must have a good sense of humor and be happy-go-lucky like her.

CAPRICORN - (December 22 - January 19) - This woman is very reserved in the beginning but once you have broken down her barriers, she will love you with all her heart with lots of intensity. She's very ambitious and career-oriented. Appeal to her by talking about making money and attaining goals.

Move slow with this woman. You must become her friend first before you can get her in the sack. She's not into casual sex, so you must not be sexually aggressive with this woman.

AQUARIUS (January 20 - February 18) - Very intelligent and you must appeal to her mind. Can be very elusive and afraid of commitment. There are a lot of bachelorettes born under this sign and they usually marry late in life.

She's a strong believer in friendship and will remain your friend even after you have broken up. Keep in mind that they can be a little cold-natured, so if you're expecting a hot & sexy passionate sex-goddess, then you may be disappointed.

PISCES (February 19 - March 20) - If you want a loving, devoted, affectionate, sympathetic woman to cater to your every need, this is the woman for you.

This woman needs lots of affection and attention. The more romance you can give her the better! She's got lots of love to give in return. She's very emotional and moody, so you will have to help keep her balanced emotionally.

67. How To Be More Affectionate With Your Girlfriend

If your relationship has taken a turn for the worse and you just don't seem to have any spark left then perhaps it's time you became more affectionate with your girlfriend before she calls things off. A new relationship is always full of affection and fun but as you become more comfortable with one another the new relationship' effort wears off. When this honeymoon period is over if you're not careful the relationship can go stale.

The honeymoon period being over isn't a bad thing because now you are comfortable with one another and can really get to know each other better. This is the period when you start acting more natural and not just trying to impress each other all the time. This is when you get to know the real person you are dating and that is great!

But.....

If you're not careful you can forget to show affection altogether and then the spark in the relationship dies. Women love affection and so if you're relationship is showing signs of going stale you need to ask yourself if you are giving her enough affection.

Being more affectionate with your girlfriend is not difficult, it's just a matter of paying attention when she speaks, showing an interest in what she says and does and contributing to the conversation. When she wants to talk to you, put the newspaper down so she knows that you are listening and that you care about what she is saying.

It is also important that if you have a bad day at work or have any issues in the relationship that you talk to her about them. It makes her feel important when you share your feelings with her and talk to her about anything that is troubling you. She will feel even more connected if you keep eye contact when she is talking to you and even hold her hand or put your hand on her knee.

Other ways that you can show your girlfriend more affection is to hold hands when you are walking down the street or along the beach. Send her flowers every now and then for no reason and just tell her that you love her. Men seem to have trouble saying the 'L' word a lot but it really makes a woman feel special when she is told that she is loved.

Affection doesn't need to be expensive and it certainly isn't hard. Even small gestures like asking her how her day was and giving her a smile when she gets home from work will mean a lot to her.

Take her out to dinner from time to time or perhaps cook her a meal.

Some men mistake affection for spending time with her but doing so with their own happiness in mind and not hers. For example, instead of taking her out for a nice quiet dinner you take her to the pub for dinner where you know all your mates will be hanging out.

Or perhaps instead of walking up behind her and wrapping your arms around her and kissing her neck, you wrap your arms around her to grab certain parts of her body without her permission. Although this may seem playful or sexy to you, it may not to her. Grabbing her in intimate parts of the body in a sleazy way or even when she's just not in the mood will make her feel degraded.

So when you are trying to become more affectionate to your girlfriend make sure that the affection is targeted at her and at making her happy. Just make her feel special and loved and you will soon see that spark return to your relationship.

68. Use this System to Succeed with Women

I would like to share my secrets on taking action to approach single women that you are interested in meeting and getting to know on an intimate basis.

I'm sure this has probably happened to you. You see a gorgeous woman that you'd give anything to meet and get to know. All you've got to do is approach her and introduce yourself. But, something holds you back. You procrastinate and put it off. Then, before you know it, she disappears and you've lost your opportunity to meet her because you didn't act fast enough.

There's a good solution to this problem of not taking action if you will do what I did to overcome procrastination when it came to approaching single women immediately that I was attracted to. Follow these steps and you will be much more successful with women:

The secret to getting things done is taking action. And you need to take action immediately when you see an opportunity to meet women that you are attracted to. You must not stall, ponder, and worry about whether she will accept your advances. You've got to approach her then and there or you may have lost a golden opportunity to make your wildest dreams come true.

And to motivate yourself to take action you need to ingrain in your subconscious mind these three words, DO IT NOW! You need to program your subconscious mind to react to these words that you repeat to yourself, which will direct your conscious mind to take action to meet women.

Repeat in your mind, DO IT NOW! And then follow up by approaching women immediately! With practice, you will develop the habit of approaching women right on the spot without hesitation. But, I must warn you that you've got to back up these words when you say, DO IT NOW! You've got to do it! If you don't, these words will be meaningless.

Trust me guys, this system works. Memorize these words, DO IT NOW! They can do wonders for your love life. Once you train your mind to approach women immediately after saying to yourself, DO IT NOW!, meeting single women will be so much easier.

It will become automatic. No more mulling over and over in your mind if you should approach that hot & sexy beautiful woman that you are attracted to. You just take action and do it after you say to yourself, DO IT NOW!

In closing, I would highly recommend that you write in big bold letters on the back of a business card, DO IT NOW! Put these cards where you will see them daily. Put one on your desk, tape one to your bathroom mirror, put one on your nightstand, tape one to your car visor or middle of your steering wheel, etc.

By seeing these three words constantly you can connect them in your mind to taking immediate action to approach and meet single women. Also, I recommend that when you see these three words that you visualize yourself approaching and meeting women.

Ok, the rest is up to you. I've given you a great system to get you up off your ass to take action to approach and meet single women. Try this system and I'd love to hear about your success stories after using the DO IT NOW! System.

69. Were You Cheated On By Your Dating Partner?

If so, what happens now? Are you going to throw the dating relationship into the trash can? Are you going to become so jaded you will never trust any one you date again? Are you so disillusioned that you want to swear off of dating relationships completely?

If you answered yes to any of the above questions, it may be time for you to take a step back and examine what is happening in your life. Even though you may have been part of the problem or more likely you weren't part of the problem, you need to know the circumstances that led to the cheating in order for you to move on with your romantic relationships or pick up the torch again for the one who cheated.

1. Has your lover's sexual advances taken a pretty sharp decline, both in the bedroom and out of the bedroom? Does he/she no longer hold your hand or put their arm around you when you're together in private or in public? Have they locked their cell phone where you can no longer answer it? These are some of the most tell-tale signs that your lover may well be involved in cheating on you. However before jumping into accusations you need to examine the evidence closely. Make sure there is not a logical reason for all of the above "cheating tell tale signs."

One of the most common things that can cause the above behavior is a physical illness or perhaps way more common, is a change in mental health. We aren't talking about becoming a sociopath, but about someone who has sank into a mild or deep depression.

If you have never been in a true depression it may be hard for you to believe that it can change someone from a full time lover to a cheating lover and worse yet; not a lover at all. His/her depression can drive your lover into the arms of someone else hoping they can find "happiness" within someone else's arms.

Unfortunately it is a fact of life and it can happen at any time.

2. Are you seeing sudden and very sharp mood swings, you have never seen before? Once again it can be part of depression or it can really be a guilty conscience because they are cheating.

Oftentimes when the mood swings occur it is because they may feel your questions are getting too close to the truth. It also can be a way they are trying to blame you for the relationship cheating. If they are a good manipulator they have learned the ways to force you into believing it's all your fault.

Mood swings can be the great deflector when your partner is feeling trapped.

If the mood swings continue, especially when the mood swing goes into "anger overload", you need to be very, very observant. These types of mood swings can quickly move from "angry" to violence.

Don't even hesitate to get out of the room or better still get completely away from where the incident is occurring. Call the police if they have assaulted you.

The above things are true signs of a "cheating dating relationship".
You need to learn them and how to deal with them.

70. Obsessive Women

"...a woman could fool herself about her relationship with a man
only as long as he was around. The moment he had left, she would
drop all pretense, and no wonder; at that moment her heart would
break and that awful, awful sickness begin: the agony, the hopeless
yearning with every fiber of her body, every nerve, for his
presence his touch; her every waking thought, her every dream
would be centered on him in unbearable, self-inflicted torture. Jan
de Hartog, "The Peaceable Kingdom"

She pursues you relentlessly. The woman will not let you alone.
She embarrasses you in public places by inappropriate displays of
affection. She calls at inopportune times and turns up at your door
without warning. She interrupts your work and intrudes into your
private business. Her professed "love" for you complicates your
life. Your devoted admirer has become an annoyance, a damned
nuisance, a scourge.

Having a woman completely enthralled by you, obsessed with you,
totally and entirely "in your power" is the stuff of fantasy, and
adolescent fantasy at that. Certainly, having a woman "hanging all
over you" might be flattering to your ego, but, for all that, it is an
unhealthy state of affairs, a dubious way to run a relationship, a
highly mixed blessing. It demeans the woman, distracts you from
attending to your life's work, and drains your energy. It might well
bring ruin upon the woman... and upon the object of her affections,
you.

71. Sometimes You Need to Analyze What You are Doing Wrong

Sometimes your dating life will get tough and you will find
yourself constantly failing to succeed with women. It seems like
everything that you do turns to crap.

When this happens, you need to look inward and do a self-analysis of what's going on in your life and why you keep striking out with women. You need to ask yourself some hard questions as to why your personality and behavior is turning women off. After all you are accountable as to what is happening or not happening in your love or sex life.

Don't fall into the trap of denying or placing blame on others as to why your dating life is in the doldrums. Don't keep saying to yourself, "This shouldn't be happening to me. I'm such a great guy and women should be falling all over me."

Accept the fact that it is happening and map out a strategy to correct it. Deal with it!

Chances are, it's your negative behavior that is turning women off. You're doing something to scare them away. I'm sure if you will do a self-analysis and take a long hard look at yourself, you will discover these negative personality and behavior traits that are turning women off. Once you discover what these are, you can take steps to eliminate them from your life. Replace them with positive traits that attract single women and you will be succeeding with women beyond your wildest dreams.

72. Women Who Dodge Your Kisses

Let me give you an example of what I mean about women dodging kisses:

You're on your first date and at some point during the date or at the end of the date you make an attempt to kiss her on the lips. However, she turns her head away and your attempt fails. At this point, don't keep trying, because you will only make her feel uncomfortable and angry with you.

So, why is she rejecting your attempt to kiss her?

1. It can be as simple as her rule to not kiss on the first date. Respect her rule if this is the case.

2. She may not want to kiss you because she is not attracted to you yet.

3. She may think you are moving too fast for her for kissing too soon.
4. She may want to get to know you better before she will allow you to kiss her.

To sum it up, if she turns her head when you try to kiss her, don't force the issue, especially on a first date. Just try and kiss her again on your next date.

Be patient guys, once you develop some chemistry, there will be lots of kissing and intimacy. Nature will take its course.

73. How to Recognize Character Flaws in a Woman

Character flaws in a woman:

- Cruelty, viciousness, as expressed in mockery, put downs.
- Immaturity, as expressed in "games playing", blame laying, whining.
- Superficiality, as expressed in vanity, flightiness, pettiness.
- Lacking in intelligence.
- Lacking in wisdom and common sense.
- Lacking in integrity and basic honesty.
- Lacking in compassion and generosity.
- Lacking in inner strength (courage).
- A woman displaying one or more of these traits has a flawed personality, and may be considered an undesirable partner.

Becoming involved with the wrong person equals a prescription for unhappiness. The adage that "it is better to have loved and lost than never to have loved at all" is scant comfort to the man courting a woman who does not return his affections. This is the dreaded "one-way love" scenario*. Nearly as nerve wracking to deal with is the woman who is not quite sure that she loves you, who plays up to you when you start to distance yourself, yet pulls away when you want closeness. Every variety of games playing, every deviation from honesty and integrity undermines a relationship at its very foundations and diminishes the people involved.

74. Eye Contact with Women

Do shivers of fear run down your spine at the prospect of communion, eye to eye, with the woman you are perhaps fated to love? Does panic freeze your limbs when you picture standing transfixed in her gaze, revealed in all your shyness and anxiety, naked and trembling? Consider then the rewards of unveiling a

new world, a jewel of creation, the realm of your darling... for is she not, like each of us, the center and shaper of her own universe? If the eyes are windows on the soul, then is not losing yourself in the countenance of your beloved the most intimate of contact? "He who looks outward sleeps, he who looks inward wakes." ---by Jung

Awaken in self-knowledge, for only then can you look upon others with the confidence of personal destiny. Mirroring the purity of intent, your look caresses, it is a reaching across, a subtle almost-touch, a sharing, a joining. The meeting of the eyes begins in almost accidental glances, intermittent, the shy but knowing smiles, an almost hesitant conversation in glimpses that recapitulates the ancient children's ritual of peek-a-boo, yet more intensely... and finally, finally (perhaps), comes that painfully delicious moment of recognition when everything clicks into sharp focus.

A warm look may hold the promise of a kiss, and more, much more. Yet, beware! Crude and untimely gawking may crush and bruise the delicate flower of a woman's private self. An intrusive stare, the "fish eye", peering, probing, clumsy goggling... all these bear the stink of an aggressive, blundering fool. Mark well that sensitivity and a delicate touch are as needful in this endeavor as in any other involving personal relationships. Mastering the gentle art of look-touching might just unlock the cage of aloneness.

Your eyes will twinkle, return smile for smile, warmth for warmth, to the woman whose regard you have captured. Words lie, facial expressions deceive, but the language of the eyes does not lend itself to falsehood. The eyes speak mutely, but they speak truly.

75. Can Your Senior Friends Help You Meet Someone New

Often when we wonder how we are going to meet a new partner, we forget about our senior friends. They will have plenty of other friends and acquaintances, one of which may be perfect for us. Yes I know, you are thinking well if they had, they would have already introduced them to me. But it doesn't always work like that.

Sometimes our friends are too embarrassed to get involved for fear that they would insult us. Not everyone likes matchmaking and your friends may not know what your views are. They may not want to jeopardize their friendship with you by meddling in your affairs. They may think that you are single through choice rather than life events and haven't thought about matching you up romantically.

Also they may decide that should they introduce you to a friend of theirs and you two subsequently became involved, they may be blamed if it didn't work out. Worse they could risk losing two friends and so rather than take that risk they don't say anything.

So it may be up to you to broach the subject with your friends. You do not need to imply that you are looking for the next Mr. or Mrs. Instead you could say that you are fed up of being on your own and would love to meet a like minded person to share some good times with. Tell them you want to go dancing or to a show and it is so much nicer to share these experiences with someone else.

It is totally up to you whether you want to give your friends some guidelines on what you are looking for in a partner. If you don't like smokers now would be a good time to mention this. Also if you are allergic to cats, it is highly unlikely you will find long term love with their friend who owns ten of these delightful creatures.

Keep it casual for now. You do not want to give your friends the impression that you are desperate and would date anyone. They know you as a person so maybe you should trust their judgment as to whom they think would be a compatible match.

Be prepared though for countless dinner invitations where you and your "date" for the evening may appear to be part of the entertainment. Your friends are not amusing themselves at your expense. But when we introduce two of our mutual friends with a view to a romantic encounter, we can often get carried away with the romance and forget that we are dealing with two people who are possibly embarrassed and more than a little nervous. Most senior couples have been together a long time so have forgotten what it is like to be single and on that first important date.

Go on, give your senior friends matchmaking services a try - after all what is the worst that could happen?

76. The Leap of Faith into Christian Singles Dating

For devout Christians, entering the dating scene can often be a confusing and sometimes unsettling experience. Let's face it, there are lots of things for the average dater to be concerned about when trying to find a suitable partner, but when it comes to Christian singles dating, matters can become even more complicated.

Despite being interested in establishing a long-term relationship with another like minded person, some Christians are afraid to barely even dip their toes into the dating pool. For some, the fear that "it can be a jungle out there" is a concern that paralyzes them, but that too common fear is more than likely largely unfounded.

While advances in technology such as online matchmaking services have made the dating experience more convenient and efficient for many people, when it comes to Christian singles dating, tradition cannot be overlooked as a factor in a single person's attitudes toward meeting other like minded singles.

It can be difficult to put aside religious convictions when venturing out into the dating world, but in fact it isn't at all necessary. For most devout Christians, finding a person of similar religious beliefs is important because so much of their makeup is based on the way they were raised or taught. A strong religious foundation more than likely comes with a strong family presence and influence, so Christian singles dating other singles will likely find themselves having to satisfy their own attraction as well as satisfying their family's expectations of who they choose in a mate. Of course, if dating another Christian single, those expectations are likely shared, or at the very least well understood.

Religious upbringing can be looked upon as both a positive and a negative when it comes to dating.

From the positive side, a person with a strong religious foundation is likely to be grounded and firm in how they approach the world and issues they face along the way. Their faith provides a strong base from which they've grown their values and morals. Christian singles dating programs certainly exist online as well as offline, and many single Christians choose to explore their dating options through the help of technology. However, many Christians still rely on the old traditional ways to meet other singles. That means their local church and church groups may be their primary way of meeting other Christian singles.

Conversely, those who are uncompromising in their Christian beliefs can, at times, be considered uncompromising or inflexible. That means that they may be considered too picky by some who don't understand just how important their religious beliefs are in establishing the person who they've become. In a nutshell, Christian singles dating options may be narrower than the general dating population, but that doesn't mean the quality of dating prospects is any less. In fact, Christian singles dating within their own set of beliefs may find that their relationships have a richness that others don't have the pleasure of experiencing.

77. How to Help Women Deal with Stress

This week I want to focus on helping women deal with stress.

Having stress in your life is just a fact of life. There is just no escaping it. We all have problems and stress.

Women and men deal with stress and problems differently. And if you know the secrets of helping women deal with stress, you will attract more women because you know how to soothe their emotions.

Let me explain the secrets to attracting single women by helping them deal with stress:

Women like to deal with their problems by talking about them repeatedly. Therefore, if you're on a date or in a relationship and she starts venting her problems, here's how to deal with it to make a good impression on her:

1. Listen...listen...listen! Let her vent and get things off her chest. Just listen and look at her right swear in the eyes. Act like you're truly concerned about her problems. Fake it if you have to. She needs you to listen to help her deal with her stress.

2. While she's venting her problems, don't interrupt her with your solutions. All she wants is for someone to listen to her and sympathize with her.

3. Whatever you do, don't tell her:

- "Get over it."
- "It's no big deal."
- "Calm down."
- "Chill out."

This is not what she wants to hear and may ever piss her off.

There you have it. If you follow these three important steps you help her deal with stress and you will be a lot more popular with single women.

78. Being Aggressive with Women

Aggressiveness

Behold the man, the man of action, the ruthless hero of myth and saga, society's darling. Here is this rugged doer of deeds, the rough-and-ready "go getter", the one who grabs what he wants without pausing to think... the aggressive stranger, the cowboy, the soldier, the gangster. Contemptuously, he shoves past that quiet guy in the corner, the shy one, the one ridiculed by family and friends as a "wimp", a "mouse", a victim, as perhaps something less than a man.

Only a nuance, a subtle shade of meaning separates aggressiveness from its less respectable cousin, aggression, the use of force to gain one's ends. With this in mind, understand aggressiveness as a sign of immaturity, of fear... of weakness, of blind stupidity. It is the crudest mode of social interaction, the blunt instrument, the bludgeon. It is the "bull in a china shop" syndrome, a behavior pattern that gets its practitioners typed as thugs, and worse. Aggressive men seem to get women, to attract women, many women, for there is something fascinating in a flame... to the hapless moth. There is an immediacy about them, a brutal spontaneity, for they recognize no tomorrow. Unfeeling, unbridled, unburdened by remorse, they leave behind them poisoned relationships, broken trust, betrayal, and despair. They loot, despoil, and ruin.

79. Dating Issues

Problems With Dating

Most dating problems occur because either the two of you are not compatible or you are not communicating enough. Other problems may be because the two of you just are not right for each other.

Communication is the most important thing when you are dating. Most problems occur because the two of you are having difficulty expressing your feelings or you aren't being clear about what you want.

When you both communicate with each other properly it is clear to

both of you if you are compatible and have the same likes and dislikes.

You cannot force a relationship if the two of you are too different or you have different goals for the relationship.

It is important to communicate about what you need and want from your relationship so you both are satisfied and you are not having disagreements about things.

Another thing that can cause problems with dating is if the two of you are not compatible. Communicating properly will tell you if you are or not.

Compatibility can be difficult if one person in the relationship is needier than the other person. If one of the people wants their space and the other is very needy then it can make it difficult for dating.

Dating problems occur when communication skills are not up to par. You have to be comfortable with the person you are with so you can talk to them.

Being comfortable and being able to communicate will show you how compatible the two of you are. If you don't have these two things then you might just consider a good friendship.

80. Dumb Dating Mistakes Men Make With Women

Do you strike out with women in the romance department no matter what you do? You can even be a drop-dead good-looking guy, but unless you know what is offensive to a woman's ears, you are likely to stick your foot in your mouth and make a fool of yourself and turn off women.

With today's women you need to know what she wants and then give it to her without sounding phony. The following are some common mistakes men make when dating women that turn women off:

1. When talking to or about women, are you still living back in time and calling them babes, broads, chicks, or something even more repulsive? Always call a woman by her name! If you use these terms mentioned, you will insult and turn women completely off.

2. When out on a date, do you spend all of your time eyeing other women in the bar, nightclub, or restaurant? Don't even think for a minute that she won't notice. She will not only notice, but may be so turned off by your behavior that she may never want to see you again. Always focus all of your undivided attention on the woman you're with. Treat her like a Princess and she will make you her Prince.

3. Another common mistake men make early in a relationship with a woman is being too sexually aggressive. After just meeting a woman you don't want to come on all hot & horny and all you can focus on is jumping her bones and pawing at her body. This kind of behavior can scare women and turn them off. They usually don't like a complete stranger pawing at their bodies and making sexual overtones. Get to know her first to where she is comfortable with you and then make your physical moves (just remember that according to the Bible you must wait until marriage to have sex).

4. When talking to a woman, do you find yourself concentrating totally on her breasts? This is a real no no! Always look women in the eyes when talking to her. Believe me, if all you can do is stare at her breasts, she will catch on to it and will ditch you as soon as possible. Women don't like men who constantly stare at their breasts. In a topless club it's OK, but not when you just meet a woman or in the early stages of dating.

5. If a woman wants to be independent, let her. For instance, if she wants to change her own flat tire, let her. If she wants to open her own door, let her. If she wants to order her own food or wine, let her. Let her assert her independence. It will make a good impression on her. You're making a big mistake if you want to act Macho all the time and not let her act independent if this is what she desires.

6. Some misguided men think it's sexy and cool to brag about what a great lover they have been to their other girlfriends, about getting high on drugs, or how good they can hold their liquor. You are not impressing women with this. As a matter of fact, she will probably find that you are obnoxious and potentially dangerous.

In closing, if you are making any of these dating blunders and displaying these offensive habits, get them corrected immediately. I hate to keep pounding this into your head, but if you turn women off you are stacking the odds against yourself in successfully meeting, dating, and attracting women.

81. Long Distance Relationships

There is a lot of controversy and different opinions regarding long distance relationships. Many people will tell you that they can never work. Then, there are people who are involved in long distance relationships that will tell you that they are the best relationships they have ever been in. They would not change where they are at for anything in the world. Long distance relationships are essentially the same as any other relationship. They require the same things from both partners. So, what makes them work or fail? The most important thing in any kind of relationship is trust and communication. If you are not able to talk to the person that you are spending time with, then you have nothing. If you cannot both completely trust each other, you will never have a meaningful relationship or make it work. In a long distance relationship, communication and trust are much more paramount. You have to rely on what your partner is saying. You are not there to know exactly what is going on. The same is true for your partner. You could be telling them one thing and doing something completely different. For many long distance couples, the internet plays a huge role in their relationship.

With instant messaging programs, webcams, microphones, and email, partners are able to communicate with each other in many different ways. The internet is often much cheaper than long distance phone calls. Plus with the use of a webcam, you can actually see the person that you are talking with. You know what they are doing and you know what is going on. It makes it much more personal. Now, if you want a very real experience, get on your web cams together and then call each other on the phone. This makes it seem as if you are actually right there together. Long distance relationships require spending a lot of time together. You need to know that your partner is there for you. You are not together and cannot spend intimate time together. You have to rely on the time that you get together. This time that you are investing in each other helps to build a bond and strengthen your relationship. It makes it much more real and special. You both become closer and have a stronger desire for each other.

Long distance relationships have great potential in most circumstances. They can work and can lead to a lifetime of happiness. This does take time and it may be something that you both have to work hard to reach.

Perhaps right now, you are both at a point where you cannot leave your jobs, your homes, or anything else that is keeping you where you live. So, you live on the belief that someday that is going to change and that you will be together in real life. This does happen for people and it can turn into the best relationship that you have ever had in your life. It is all a matter of how much time you put into it and how patient and how able you are to wait for the right time to be together.

Some people have spent years in a long distance relationship before they have ever met their partner. Others are in a relationship for a few months and then they meet each other. They are not able to stay together at this point, but that short time that they have together means a great deal to both people.

82. Marriage Requirements You Must Meet To Have A Happy Marriage

This article is for single men who are getting married or thinking about getting married.

There are certain marriage requirements that must be met in order to have a strong happy relationship. If these requirements aren't met, you are going to have a long, hard time building a relationship that works. Not meeting all these marriage requirements is, in fact, the primary reason that divorce rates are so high these days.

You'd be surprised how many people's relationships don't actually meet the marriage requirements necessary for a good, solid marriage. This is all too often the result of people getting together and deciding to get married without really stopping to see if they are truly compatible.

The marriage requirements are pretty basic, and we'll get to them in a minute, but you need to keep in mind that if you come up wanting, there is something you can do about it. You don't have to write off a relationship if it doesn't meet all the criteria, you just need to know how to work to make it fit.

There are four basic marriage requirements, all of them important, but not all of them equally important. If you have all four of these, there's a very good chance that your marriage will be able to go the distance.

Respect – You need to have a deep and mutual respect for each other. This means that you take each other's problems and concerns seriously, and don't write each other's feelings off as frivolous or worthless. You'd be amazed how many relationships start with a shaky foundation because respect is absent.

Good Communication – One of the most important marriage requirements is the ability to talk openly and honestly with each other in a way that each of you understands exactly what the other person is saying. This is important because it will allow you to

work through most problems. Without it, you're probably going to have a failed marriage.

Common Goals – A good couple does need to have the exact same goals, but you do need to have some common goals and goals that are mutually compatible. If one of you wants to have kids and the other doesn't, this can be a serious problem. Find out early what you both want and need and you'll be able to build a marriage that lasts.

Love – Perhaps unsurprisingly, this is the most important of the marriage requirements we've discussed. It seems like a no-brainer, but you'd be surprised how many people marry out of obligation or to avoid loneliness. You need to take a good long look and make sure you really are in love and are not just trying to fill an emotional hole. If you are in love, most of the other requirements mentioned probably already exist, and if they don't, they can be developed. If you find that you are lacking in one or more of these marriage requirements, don't worry; most of them can be developed. You just need to work on it with a good solid plan in place. There are many of these available too, so just pick the right system to help you make your marriage everything it should be.

83. She's In the Army Now – Dating Service Women

When you say "soldier" a picture of a fit and ready man comes to mind. But almost 15 percent of the US. armed forces are now women. So, in many cases, when you think about military personnel, a female soldier should come to mind. Because there are now so many females in the military, there is an issue about dating service women.

Dating service women presents challenges that aren't there when you are dating a civilian. She has obligations that her non-military sisters don't have. For instance, she could suddenly be deployed to a war zone. She is also likely to be moved from base to base every couple of years. So dating service women means being prepared to follow their careers and support them when they need it.

If you are going to be dating service women, you need to know that although she is in a masculine profession (the military), she still wants to be treated like a lady. She's "one of the boys" in her work life. She wants to be all female when she is with you.

You also need to invest time learning about the military in general and her specialty specifically. This means learning the acronyms that she spouts off at the drop of a hat. This is the way she communicates, and you need to be part of that.

You should also know something about military culture. Military law governs every aspect of a service woman's life. No business can tell you that you can lose your job because of the person you date or put you in jail for something you did in your off hours. But, the military "owns" the enlisted person or officer. When dating service women, get to know the culture and the specific challenges they face.

There are times when you make plans with your girlfriend and she suddenly has to drop whatever it is you are doing and report to base. It doesn't matter whether the event is really important to you. She has no choice in whether to go to your parent's 50th wedding anniversary if she is called up on an emergency drill.

She will need you to keep her motivated. The military is still not a gender neutral place. If her career is important to her, you need to support her as she moves up the chain of command.

When dating a military woman, it is important that you support her decision to be part of the Armed Services. You may not agree with everything the military does, but she made the decision before she met you to be a part of serving her country. Unless she's Chairman of the Joint Chiefs, she doesn't have much control over military or foreign policy. Just as you wish she would be supportive of your work, you have to realize that her career is important to her.

There are many challenges in dating a service woman. But, when you fall in love with a military woman, you know a lot of things about her already. For instance, she fits into a larger organization. She's physically fit. She pays attention to details. She is probably quite loyal and dependable. And, she knows what patriotism and love of country are. You could do a lot worse than dating service women.

84. You Can Kill the Anxiety of Seniors Dating

Just because you've reached retirement age doesn't mean you've got to retire from an active social life. Mature dating is one of the hottest trends these days, especially when you consider how much more vital and healthy today's senior citizens have become. Years ago, people in their sixties may have been relegated to the old folks homes, but that isn't the case any longer. Instead, retirement aged people are enjoying a long and healthy social life, thanks to advances in health care and the fact that people are living longer, happier lives. Hey, if you're a senior and returning to an active social life for the first time in years, you may think that you've been left behind. That isn't the case at all. Even though you may feel like you're a little bit "rusty" when it comes to dating, you shouldn't hesitate to enter the mature dating scene and kick your personal relationships into high gear. To help, we're offering these three top tips for mature dating:

1. At this stage in your life the pressure is off, so don't pressure yourself. Think about it: you're an active and vital senior citizen, and these days many of the things that may have consumed much of your life are behind you. If you're retired, then you no longer face the daily grind at work, meaning you have the opportunity to explore a mature dating relationship that allows you to spend even more quality time with your potential mate. Don't pressure yourself, instead take advantage of the fact that certain pressures -- like work or career -- are now behind you.

2. Don't worry about your age. Age is nothing more than a number. You've heard the old expression that "you're as young as you feel" and that's absolutely true. Think about the fact that you have the opportunity to enjoy many, many more active years and more exciting personal relationships. When you think about putting together a date with another senior, consider doing more active things like golf or tennis or even a trip to the gym. Let's face it, no matter your age, being in great shape is important, and that goes for mature dating relationships as well.

3. Don't be afraid of technology. Computers, the Internet, cell phones, and all sorts of new technology are around us and we're exposed to it more and more every day. You'd be surprised how many people entering the mature dating scene are using technology to help them find a suitable partner. Whether it be an online dating site or simply chatting someone up via email, technology is nothing to be afraid of and in fact may help you boost your ability to attract another person.

Sixty is the new forty, and mature dating is one of the things that today's seniors can experience and enjoy. Don't be afraid to take a chance on a new relationship, and follow these three top tips to help you have success.

85. Over Sixty Dating for Sexy Senior Citizens

When it comes to senior life these days, sixty isn't what it used to be thirty years ago. It seems that as time continues to march forward, those over the age of sixty aren't being left behind. More seniors are keeping themselves in great shape, and advances in medicine and nutrition mean people are living longer and more healthy than ever. Senior citizens these days are more vital and vibrant than any of previous generations. So what if you're in the area of retirement age and you're looking for a mate? Over sixty dating can be a lot of fun and a totally rewarding experience.

Relationship expert and Internet author Wendell K. Cribbs reminds us that no matter what our age, dating and relationships are important to a healthy mental attitude and a rewarding personal life. We shouldn't allow nervousness and fear to keep us from developing healthy intimate relationships despite our age. Many of the fears seniors face when it comes to over sixty dating are fears that simply exist in their own minds.

"For people over sixty dating shouldn't be something to be afraid of," explained Cribbs. "In fact, dating for seniors can be a very exciting and fun experience. As we reach our senior years, many of the issues that face younger singles aren't nearly as significant or don't even exist at all. Things like career, family, plans for children and the like simply aren't as prominent. That means over sixty dating can be a lot more casual and a lot less restrictive with a lot less pressure."

Robert is a 66-year-old retired office manager who enjoys the over sixty dating scene, but that wasn't always the case for him. "I find dating at my age to be a lot more fun with a lot less pressure than when I was younger," he says. "Looking back on my life, I realize that I dated my wife exclusively for more than six years before we got married. I remember that everything was just so serious for us at that time. We had a great life together, and when she passed away, I felt like I may just hide in my apartment and never go out with anyone again. That feeling lasted about six months, until some of my friends finally talked some sense into me. Then I just put aside all my fears and put myself out there."

Cribbs says Robert's situation isn't uncommon for those who are entering the over sixty dating scene for the first time. "Of course there is going to be a certain level of nervousness and trepidation when it comes to dating again," the expert says. "Despite the fact that senior age people have a lot of life experience behind them, often they've spent literally dozens of years in a long-term relationship or marriage."

So seniors looking to re-establish a potential loving and fulfilling personal relationship shouldn't be worried about entering the over sixty dating process. After all, your life is what you make of it, no matter what your age.

86. Motivational Spiritual Comments

- All through the day I will meditate on these thoughts: God's love, my love for God, and his will for finding the right woman for me.
- The right opportunities to meet a very special woman are heading my way. Blessings from Jesus almighty are chasing me down in my pursuit of this woman.
- I am not lonely anymore. Things have shifted in my favor in my dating life. With Jesus's blessing I have now found the right woman for me.
- Praise Jesus! Out of nowhere the girl I have been praying for has appeared.
- Good breaks from Jesus are tracking me down in my quest for a soulmate.
- When you least expect it your dream girl can appear out of nowhere. Why? Because in the blink of an eye one touch of Jesus's favor can turn your love life around for the better.
- I'm depending on Jesus to bring me a very special lady to love. He will arrange good breaks to meet her with my name on them in my pursuit of her.
- I will keep praising Jesus with the attitude that someone good is coming my way. My days of dating the wrong women are over. Jesus has put an end to that.
- If you seek Jesus to help you in your dating life, blessings will seek after you because Jesus loves it when you ask for help and depend on him.
- I'm not staying lonely, depressed, and frustrated about my dating life.

Online Dating

This section is devoted to the highly effective way of meeting women online by answering and running personal ads online. Many men have used this method and get lots of responses from beautiful and sexy women (with photos) from lovely women from all over the United States and locally.

There are lots of lonely women out there searching for romance and companionship. Advertising is a dignified way for them to meet men and they are able to screen the men that respond through their letters, email, photos, and phone calls.

There's only going to be one drawback to this method unless you meet someone local. You will probably have to do some traveling to meet the women and this could become an expensive habit. It's well worth it if you can afford it. A lot of people have found their life mate this way. If you like to travel, you can travel all over the US meeting women you've become intimate with through correspondence and talking over the phone.

Some women will even visit you from out of state as they did me. Some even paid for all their expenses. I really had some fun times!

87. Senior Internet Dating A Whole New World

Senior internet dating has opened up a new world for people over the age of 50 who want to meet interesting people of the opposite sex. When marriages lasted for a lifetime and sex for old people was considered "icky" mature adults didn't do as much going out. But times and technology have changed everything. Now senior internet dating has hit the mainstream.

Senior internet dating has given a new lease on life for many senior citizens worldwide who are looking for love and friendship. The world wide web makes it easy to make new friends and meet love interests online. You only need a home computer and an internet connection to get started.

Then you have the potential to communicate with eligible singles from all over the world.

First, you need to select a senior online dating service. There are many to choose between so you will have to do some research to find one that offers you a good opportunity of meeting someone online. Keep in mind that along with the behemoth sites that have hundreds of thousands of members, there are smaller, more specialized sites as well. Most sites will offer you a free trial period. This way you can test the service out first so you can see just what it offers you.

This way you can test the service out first so you can see just what it offers you. Don't use any service that doesn't offer either a free trial or limited membership. They may be scams. There are plenty of senior internet dating services that allow you access without paying upfront or giving them any information about yourself.

When you have found a senior internet dating service that you feel will give you a good chance of meeting a potential date, you can create your free account. Then start browsing the profiles. At first, you'll be looking for how many senior singles you have living in your area, and how many of these singles have their photo attached to their profile. This gives you a good idea of how much chance you'll have at interacting with someone who you can meet if things work out. Also, singles who post their photo are more serious about internet dating, and you'll have a better chance of a response from them.

You should also put your picture on your profile. If you don't, you may have very limited numbers of contacts. Singles with a photo on their personal ad get 20 times more messages sent to them. The reasons are numerous but boil down to the fact that no one wants to communicate with someone who won't show their face.

Additionally, most people who use the search function search only for profiles with photographs, so you won't show up if you don't have one posted.

When you want to start sending emails, you will need to upgrade your membership. This can range from a few dollars a month to hundreds of dollars a year. However, the point of putting up a profile is to meet people, and sending emails is the way you communicate through these services.

Once you've started your senior internet dating you'll begin to enjoy it. While it might seem a bit daunting at first, everyone already on the site was in your position once. Just remember that everyone who is a member of an online dating service is there because they want to be contacted.

88. Guidelines for Online Dating

Get to Know the Guidelines

If you haven't dated online before, you should get to know some of the tips and guidelines that are generally held. While online dating has similarities to dating in person, there are also some big differences. Not only should you have an idea of online dating etiquette so you don't offend someone, you should also be able to tell when you should or shouldn't be offended by someone else's behavior.

A good example of this when you are dating singles online is that it is not only acceptable to talk to many different potential dates at once, but it is encouraged. The whole point of being online is to meet a bunch of people and talk to them. Don't be afraid to be in contact with a bunch of people.

But generally once you have begun actually dating someone, you need to put your account on hold. You don't have to do this on your first or second date, but once you decide to pursue a relationship with someone, freeze your account out of respect for them and others who don't want to date someone who may already be involved.

89. How to Attract Women on Dating Sites

The explosion of online dating sites has created a bit of a pickle for single guys looking to meet an interesting and successful woman online. Some men fear that women on dating sites misrepresent themselves, which they worry could lead to disappointment when meeting in person. While this may be true of some women, in general most females who create a serious online profile on a dating site and are looking for a legitimate dating partner will be primarily truthful in both their profiles and their photos. Women worry that men will be similarly untruthful, but likewise they should put those fears aside and (at least initially) focus on trying to find a good match and worry about potential misrepresentation later. Unfortunately, part of the problem is rooted in the different ways that men and women perceive one another and a misunderstanding of what may be the important things that lead to attraction between the sexes.

For a man to successfully attract women on dating sites, he needs to first be aware that many women are looking primarily for someone who stimulates them intellectually more than physically. While physical attraction is important to women on dating sites, being able to hold an intelligent conversation goes a long way to proving that you're an intellectual match for the female of your choice. Therefore, before you meet a woman in person for a live date, make sure you've spent plenty of time conversing with her via email and let her see that you are capable of holding her attention. Once you've established yourself as someone she can speak comfortably with, you're more likely to have success with her on a real, live date.

Remember guys, women on dating sites are pretty much the same as women you first meet in person.

And as for men, women on dating sites who are seeking a serious relationship with a man they might meet online should realize that many men are insecure about certain parts of themselves, despite putting on a brave front or a macho exterior. Like men, women on dating sites who are meeting men online should spend a good deal of time conversing via email to get a good understanding of just who he is. Look for those insecurities, and when the time comes to meet in person, you'll have a good handle on how to give him the attention he needs to help boost his confidence. A confident, self-assured man is going to typically be a more fun and engaging date for a woman than a man who is insecure and afraid.

When it comes to attracting women on dating sites, or for women seeking a dating partner among men on dating sites, the best advice is to put aside your preconceived notions or worries about potential misrepresentation and instead focus on first creating a long line of email correspondence before meeting up in person. In this way you'll get a much better idea of who you're talking with, and through that interaction make a much more informed decision about meeting for a real, live date.

90. Would A Senior Online Dating Service Work For You?

We all know that dating at any age can be daunting. But when you are a little older and perhaps fussier, a senior online dating service can be just the ticket to finding your perfect mate.

We are all living longer due to advances in our diet, medical research and our lifestyles. Our financial circumstances have improved. We are less likely to be living with our kids or grandkids. Sometimes through death or divorce, we can end up facing our senior moments alone. Some people relish the freedom this can bring but others are lonely and would love to enjoy a committed relationship.

It is fairly difficult to meet someone special when you are in your twenties and thirties. Don't believe me? Just have a glance at the book titles on the best seller lists. You will see books on finding and keeping the man/woman for you, the golden rules of dating, meeting the perfect man/woman etc.

It can often be more difficult for older people to meet potential partners. You are very unlikely to go to the local nightclub or bar.

You may find going into a restaurant or bar on your own intimidating and you are probably retired so meeting someone at work is not an option.

By joining a senior dating service, you can meet like-minded individuals of a certain age, economic status and marital status. For example, you may prefer not to date a divorced woman. Or you may prefer that your potential partner has been in a committed relationship previously. You may want the other person to share your religious or cultural beliefs. An online dating service will help you to meet someone who fulfills this "shopping list" of requirements.

When you join an online service, you need to remember that your personal safety is paramount. There is no reason to become alarmed as the majority of members on these sites are there for the same reason as you are to meet a companion. Exercise common sense and caution when dealing with anyone you don't know regardless of how friendly they seem. If you arrange to meet a prospective partner, always do so in a public place and give a friend or family member the details. Never disclose too much information about yourself particularly your home address or your financial details until you have met the other person and have formed the basis of a relationship.

You wouldn't walk into a bar and start telling another customer that you have $100,000 in your bank account. Friendships which start online can become very intense very quickly. It is partly because we lose our inhibitions and can be ourselves without worrying about what we look like or how tall we are etc. But you do not know someone until you have met them and become familiar with them.

Senior online dating services work - you only need to ask some of their satisfied customers. Try them out today as your Mrs. right may be online now.

91. Online Dating Advice For Men: The Online Personal Ad

Do you think that online dating is only for nerds or misfits? Think again. It's estimated that over 12 million women visit online dating sites every month looking for their perfect match.

The internet is changing many aspects of the past as we know it and one of those is dating. On-line dating services have become the latest and greatest craze, with both men and women rushing to the web to find their "matches" or read their admirors's emails via an internet connection rather than communicating in the old-fashioned upfront and personal way.

Online sources like eHarmony and Lavalife boast that they "match up" happy couples so successfully that many of them promise a match within six months of joining their services. The following online dating advice for men will start from the beginning. . .how to create your first online personal ad.

The first concept you need to grasp in creating your personal ad is that you will have a lot of competition. So you need to make sure that you stand out from the crowd. You want to be unique and as specific as possible. Also, if you can establish a sense of urgency, that's an extra added touch. This means conveying a message that you will not be around waiting forever.

Think of your personal ad as a sales page. . .for yourself. So, you'll have a headline, your personal profile and a close which guarantees the "sale."

Start with the headline. This is the most important part so make it good. Studies have shown you have three seconds to capture the attention of whoever is reading your headline. A great way to do this is to ask a question. . .something that gets the reader to think.

The next step is your profile. This is where many men need this online dating advice for men because they get this part wrong. In the profile, you will write about what you do and don't like, your activities, etc. Anyone can say that they like reading, traveling, swimming, etc. Instead, write in detail about one of your favorite places or a place that you are planning to visit in the near future. This stimulates your next date's senses.

In the close of your profile, let your readers know that you will be off again soon (maybe to one of those interesting places you mentioned in your profile).

Here are a couple of general points to keep in mind when preparing your profile. Make sure it is grammatically correct. If it isn't, you will appear either stupid or lazy. Next, only three out of every 10 men who post a personal ad on a dating site get a response. This is because most men's ads are boring, repetitive or filled with errors.

92. Are Online Relationships Good Or Bad

If you've met someone online you may be wondering, are online relationships good? For the most part, that depends on the exact nature of the relationship and how each of the people in the relationship feels about it.

Relationships are very personal and every person, and couple, to some degree make their own rules. Having said that though, most good relationships will have some common features.

For instance, it's important at an early stage for each of you to discuss what you want to get out of the relationship. Now, obviously, I'm not talking about pledging your undying love after you've just met someone, but as you get to know one another if the bond seems to be growing, would either, or both, of you like to eventually meet? Or would you be more comfortable just keeping things in the cyber world?

There is no right or wrong when it comes to that question, but it's important that you are both on the same page. Someone can get hurt if they feel the connection is strong enough to warrant actually meeting in person and the other person has no desire to take the relationship that far.

If one or the other of you is using your online relationship to cheat on a real world partner, then it's not really good. Cheating is cheating and most people would define it as having an emotional connection, a romantic connection, with someone other than your partner. Even if the two of you never meet and never have a physical relationship, many would consider it cheating to have another romantic love besides your partner.

One of the biggest things everyone has to remember when they are involved in an online relationship of any kind is that you don't really know for sure who you're talking to. That 21 year old female college student from Kansas may actually be a 45 year old plumber from Pittsburgh. Yikes! It's hard to really form a bond with another person if you can't even be sure who they really are.

Online relationships allow you to fill in a lot of the blanks about a person, and more often than not you'll fill things in the way you would like them to be. This may be one of the biggest pitfalls of all when it comes to online relationships. Of course, if the two of you actually meet in person, you will overcome that obstacle. But if the two of you are content to leave things strictly online you have to remember that you can only get so close to someone when you can't ever be sure they are who they say they are.

Many people would argue that you can never really get to know another person, but if you've actually met them in person at least you know to some degree, if they are really who they say they are.

All in all the question: are online relationships good depends largely on you and what you're looking for in a relationship. The internet offers a great way to meet new people, just make sure that you are clear about what it is you are really looking for.

93. 5 Benefits of Dating Singles Online

If you are looking for companionship, then you are now, or soon to be, counted among the growing number of dating singles online.

Dating websites are more popular than ever, and still growing. There are several reasons why this is the case, some of which may surprise you.

1. Trying something new. It doesn't take long for single people to get tired of the traditional dating scene. It's either too boring, time-consuming or otherwise demanding. When dating singles online the problems of traditional dating virtually disappear. Sure, you still have to sort through several people, but the way the "hunt" is conducted is entirely different.

2. Convenience. You don't have to spend a lot of time getting ready when dating online. All you have to do is log in to the dating website of your choice, look at profiles, and maybe exchange a few messages. This takes much less time than getting dressed up and driving somewhere. If all goes well, you will eventually meet someone face-to-face, but until then, you don't have to worry about the normal inconveniences.

3. A large pool. No, this isn't referring to a nice place to swim. Rather, it refers to the fact that there is a large pool of potential dating partners available online. After all, you are connecting to people from all over (though there are sites that cater to smaller areas). You no longer have to choose from the same dozen or so regulars at your local singles bar. Instead, you may have access to thousands and thousands of profiles.

4. Variety. Maybe you live in a small town and love the works of Voltaire, professional wrestling, scrapbooking and Czech cheeses. It may be nearly impossible to find anyone in your area that shares those interests. With the massive variety of dating online singles, your chances of finding someone with the same tastes goes up significantly. Of course, those with more standard tastes are out there, too.

5. Anonymity. But isn't the whole idea of online dating to get to know someone? It is, but by being anonymous early on, you can feel more at ease being yourself. When somebody isn't looking at your profile, it doesn't feel like they are giving you the cold shoulder. It's not you as a person they aren't responding to, it's the data contained in your profile. Also, if you happen to get rejected, you won't take it as personally because you are not as emotionally invested. Rejection works both ways, though, and online dating takes care of that problem, too. If you aren't interested in somebody, all you need to do is move on to another profile; all without the fear of guilt.

Traditional dating isn't going away, but with all it has going for it, online dating is becoming a more and more serious competitor. Oh, and the best thing of all? The chance to meet somebody special and be happy.

94. Personal Ads

Why, Oh Why Would a Woman Respond to a Personal Ad?

- The ad intrigues her. She wants to find out more about this person whose words bring a bloom to her cheeks, make her blood fizz, and set her off daydreaming.
- The ad speaks to her, personally. "Hey, this is me, he's looking for me!"
- The ad illuminates an overcast winter day, makes her laugh, fall silent, then dissolve in tears.
- The ad presents the type of fellow she would seriously consider for a long term relationship as a lover, a mate, a friend.
- The ad comes into her life at just the right time, just when she's looking for someone like you. Fortune smiles.
- For no particular reason she can put a name to it. It just feels right.

95. Computer Dating Advice for Men

The Do's And Dont's Of Computer Dating

Computer dating can be a great way to meet people who are compatible with your interests. It can allow non-threatening introductions, and let you meet lots of others. Sometimes it develops long term relationships.

While computer dating is very popular and generally safe, you should take some precautions. Dating is, by definition, a personal thing, and you should be cautious about giving out personal information online.

Choosing a reputable service is the first step you'll want to take. Talk to friends about sites they've had good experiences with. See if any of the couples you know met online.

It's also important to check out the reviews of computer dating services. You won't want to make a judgment from one review. But if you keep reading the same complaints over and over, you'll likely want to avoid the site.

One of the great benefits of computer dating is that you can meet people from all over that have the same interests that you have. If you have an unusual hobby, you can specify that in your profile. If you want to meet others of the same faith, you can join sites especially for your faith.

After you choose a site and post a profile, you may have people request a contact. You may see others you'd like to meet. Just take it very slowly at first. Initiate a conversation, but keep your information anonymous.

You should have lots of online conversations before you set up a face-to-face meeting. Be very discriminating about continuing relationships. If there are any red flags, you'll want to proceed very cautiously or end the relationship before meeting. You don't need to invite excess drama into your life, and you want to stay safe.

Set realistic expectations about the people you meet. You are likely going to date several people who don't work out. Statistics tell us that many of those you meet will be people you never want to see again. Others won't want to see you again!

Don't be discouraged if things don't work out. Recognize that part of the experience is the journey. You're meeting people and finding out what works for you and what doesn't. If the next person has the same qualities you liked in the first, but likes you, too, you're onto something.

It's best to be reasonable about long distance relationships from the beginning. Are you willing to commit to flying across the country every week? Driving 50 miles and back several times a week? It can be done, but be sure you are really prepared to make that commitment.

Take it slowly. Sometimes we think we know someone because we've connected online, but we don't really know him or her at that point. Don't agree to something unwise, like going on a cruise with someone you've never met.

Be yourself. Computer dating is not the place to present a new you or try to reinvent who you are.

It's the time to find someone with whom the real you can connect over the long term.

96. Christian Dating Sites What Does Your Future Hold

Have you been looking for the perfect man or woman to compliment your life and share your earthly journey with? Are you having difficulty finding that person? If you have not had much success on your own, you really should consider Christian dating sites.

What does your future hold? Do you see yourself enjoying a rich, rewarding life with someone who shares your faith in the Lord? If it is your goal to have such a blessing and you are ready to start sharing time and love with another person, it makes sense to employ the assistance of Christian dating sites.

What does your future hold? Are you worried that your perfect partner has been so well hidden that you will never find him or her? It does often seem as if it is impossible to find a lasting, loving relationship. Some of us search our whole lives, and we go out to singles' bars (that is just a waste of time), look around at church on Sunday mornings, endure blind dates set up by well-meaning friends, and all the rest, but still our perfect match eludes us. Perhaps it is time to try Christian dating sites.

What does your future hold? Do you dream of falling in love and finding that one person with whom you were meant to share life? Christian dating sites can help you avoid the pitfalls that traditional dating can often present. Christian dating sites can help you find people with similar interests. If you want an outdoorsy type, Christian dating sites can help you find her. If you prefer a homebody who loves to make Italian food, Christian dating sites can help you find her. What does your future hold? Time spent alone and going out on blind date after blind date only to be disappointed yet again? You do not have to settle for that. Christian dating sites can help you find the perfect person for you.

Many people may not think that online dating is too great an idea; maybe you yourself have considered it but have thought it a little too "weird." Well, technology has brought us a million more ads for things we don't need, and no one fusses too much about that. Technology has brought us insane amounts of adult material that does nothing but harm individuals and society.

Technology has brought us a way to distance ourselves from the outside world by sitting alone in our bedrooms and living rooms and staring at a monitor. Technology has brought us online gossip about celebrities and places for teenagers to show pictures of themselves that show too much. Technology has brought us the ability to be reached by phone all day every day, even in church a lot of the time. Technology has brought kids a way to tune out the teacher and tune in the tunes with tiny earpieces and tiny MP3 music holders.

Isn't it time that technology brought us what we really want and need – a special person to love? Of course it is. It is time. Christian dating sites: what does your future hold?

97. Avoid The Perils of Online Dating For Seniors

Finally, online dating for seniors has given us a real way of meeting potential life partners. Forget joining the local aged veterans club, or the cookery course for the over 55 or Yoga for the mature age group. Now you can join a website and within minutes have access to a group of individuals who are looking for partners and actually know who Bob Hope and John Wayne were.

Ok so that last comment was meant as a joke. But seriously mention online dating clubs to most people, of a certain age, and they automatically think you are trying to hook up with a twenty five year old.

Online dating for seniors opens up a world of opportunity that generations before us couldn't dream of. Not only can you find someone who has the qualities you admire most but the fact that they are a member means that they are also looking for someone special.

So how do you find your Mrs Right? Well there is no "fail safe way" but it helps if you give the process a chance. Despite what the movies may say, less than a quarter of happily married women "knew" that the man they were dating was the "one" on the first couple of dates. Love is like a delicate flower - it needs time and attention to mature to its full promise. So the moral of the story is that you should give a new friendship time to mature. Unless of course, you are obviously incompatible.

Using an online service allows you to build up friendships via email or instant messenger before you have to talk to the person. Often, probably due to the anonymity, we get closer quicker to people we have only met on email than we would if we meet them in person.

When preparing for your first date, think about the first impression the other person is going to get. If it has been a while since you were out socially, you may be stuck in a time warp. I'm not suggesting you need to become a fashion victim but get a good friend to vet the outfit you choose; to double check the image you are projecting. Mutton dressed as lamb is never attractive for either sex!

Make sure that you stick to the following rules when using any dating service. Until you have complete trust in the other person i.e. have met in person and preferably more than once.

1) Communicate via the agency's internal secure email system. Do not give out your home or cell number, or your full name and address.

2) Always meet in a public place.

3) Always, always have your own transportation home. Get a friend, family member or have a taxi booked for a specific time to collect you.

Abide by these simple rules and you will have no problems avoiding the perils of online dating for seniors. Who knows, it could turn into an enjoyable way to spend an evening or two. Or it may turn into a lifetime commitment for both of you.

More Dating Advice

98. How to Win Love Back

Learning how to win love back may be able to reignite a burned out relationship. Love is a truly fickle emotion that can burn out just as quickly and suddenly as it was originally ignited. When outside factors, such as money for example, create stress in a relationship that love is most at risk. Once relationship problems become an issue, love can quickly deteriorate with no resolution in sight. Here are some basic strategies that will show you how to win love back:

* **Be Honest** - Distrust is one of the leading causes of problems in a relationship. It is extremely important that you are honest with your partner on every possible level, even in situations where the truth is painful. This means that you need to be upfront with things that are bothering you, and you also need to be open about everyday activities like finances and how you are doing at work. No one likes to feel like they constantly have to watch over their significant other, so if you want to learn how to win love back, you need to make a commitment to honesty.

* **Be Encouraging** - Love is all about appreciating one another for who you are and this is a big step in learning how to win love back. Your partner may have different goals and interests than you. The key is to embrace them even if you do not agree with them, and support them with all of your heart. Encourage growth in your partner's interests, and you will be promoting growth in your relationship.

* **Be Dependable** - Being dependable is an important part of rebuilding trust with your partner, and learning how to win love back. When you want to learn how to win love back, you need to learn how to follow through with the promises that you make, and you need to make an effort to be on time with the appointments that you make.

* **Listen Actively** - Communication is one of the most vital ingredients in every healthy relationship, so if you want to learn how to win love back, you need to learn how to communicate more

effectively. Not only does this mean that you need to learn how to speak better, but also learn how to listen better as well. This is one of the true keys to learning how to win love back, and no relationship is solid without healthy and proactive communication.

* **Act!** - Keep in mind that all relationships have ups and downs, even the best ones. If you want to learn how to win love back, you need to be willing to learn how to take action and repair the problems in our relationship. You cannot simply sit back and wait for the relationship problems to go away on their own, as this will make your partner feel alienated more than anything. So if you are ready to learn how to win love back, take the aforementioned advice to heart and take action once and for all.

99. Problems - Short Timers

There are those single women that are just fine dating once, twice or maybe three times and then bail out suddenly. While you can't predict this behavior, you can understand it when it happens. In this way you can deal with it. Your best strategy is to let it go. You are only one in a series of men who have played her game. It's not about you. It's about her and her problems. Move on.

- She may be in love with the concept of falling in love. Then she doesn't know what to do with it.
- She may have been hurt badly in a previous relationship. She can't bring herself to get serious.
- She may thoroughly enjoy dating men - lots of men - often. It was just your turn.
- What if you are the one who exhibits these behaviors? That is a serious problem. You will never pass go and collect two hundred dollars if you don't figure out what is wrong. You may need to get some good professional help. However, you can try some of these suggestions to get past the problem.
- Do something about it. If you don't see a strategy here that helps, resolve to find a way to turn the situation around. You are after all playing mind games with yourself. You know yourself better than anyone, or at least you should.
- Try to figure out why. Have you ever had a committed

relationship? Did something painful happen? What about during your childhood? Did you have a good relationship with your parents and your siblings?

- Stay in the moment. Deal with her in the present. Don't try to project what might happen in the future if you continue to see her. Also, your potential with her is completely unknown and not related to your past.
- Stretch yourself. Make a good-faith attempt to continue dating her past your usual cut-off point. This will negate ingrained behavior patterns you have developed as a defense.
- Give the new situation a chance. This woman is new in your life. She has nothing to do with any painful episodes in your past. Any comparisons or similarities you are drawing are of your own design. Try to put things in their proper time perspective. That was then - this is now.

100. The Best Way to Ask Single Women Out on a Date

The way you ask for a date with single women can make a big difference in whether she accepts or declines. Also, it's very important that you feel confident in advance that she is going to accept your invitation to get together for a date.

Whatever you do, don't expect a "no" answer in advance of asking her out. This can backfire on you by showing the woman your lack of confidence around women. If you expect rejection, it can create a self-fulfilling prophecy.

Let me give you some examples of the wrong way of asking single women for a date. These negatively phrased questions can set you up for failure in trying to get a date:

"I know you're probably busy Friday night, but if you're not busy would you like to go out with me?"

"I don't suppose you're free to have lunch with me on Friday are you?"

"You wouldn't want to meet me for a drink Thursday after work, would you?"

Can you see how negative these questions are? They are already programmed for a "no" answer. Plus, she might think that you have already asked someone else out and you got shot down, so now you are trying your luck with her. Her thinking this, even though it might not be true, puts you in a bad position.

It's best to make it easy for the woman you're asking out to accept your invitation for a date. Make it easy for them to say, "yes." Also, think positive when asking her out. Believe that she is going to accept and there's no way that she will say, "no."

In my opinion, here's the best way to ask a woman for a date:

"My friends have been raving about a new Italian restaurant that serves really great food. I've never been there. Would you like to try it out with me?" (This really doesn't have to be the truth, just make it up to get a date).

"There's a good symphony/play coming to town in a couple of weeks. This sounds like a really fun thing to attend. Would you like to join me?"

"Some of my friends are going to the beach this weekend to hang out and party. They have asked me to come along. I know it would be a lot of fun. Would you like to come along with me?"

I'm sure you get the idea now. These are non-pressured and direct questions for asking for a date. They sound so much better than the negative examples I gave you to not use for asking for a date. Don't you agree?

I hope this advice helps you to get more dates and happy hunting!

Bonus Section:

How to Use the Power of Prayers to
Meet, Date, and Attract Women

If you are not a Christian and do not believe in God or Jesus these prayers will not help you. They will fall on deaf ears because you have turned your back on God and Jesus. To become a new born Christian I encourage you to say this simple prayer to receive salvation through Jesus and become a Christian:

God in heaven, I come to you admitting that I am a sinner. Right now, I choose to turn away from sin, and I ask You to cleanse me of all unrighteousness. I believe that Your only begotten Son, Jesus, who was born of the virgin Mary, died on the cross to take away my sins. I also believe that He rose again from the dead so that I might be forgiven of my sins and made righteous through faith in Him. I call upon the name of Jesus Christ to be Savior and Lord of my life. Jesus, I choose to follow You and ask that You fill me with the power of the Holy Spirit. I declare right now I am a child of God. I am free from sin and full of the righteousness of God. Thank you, Lord. My life is now completely in your hands and I will live for You who gave Yourself for me that I may live forever. I am saved in Jesus' name. Amen.

Welcome to the family of God! If you know other believers, be sure and share this exciting news with them. Also, join a local Bible-based church to connect and worship with other followers of Jesus Christ. There are lots of beautiful and love-hungry women out there dying to meet you and the following prayers will help you find and attract them and fill your life with lots of love, romance, and good times using the power of Jesus:

My Prayer: "Dear God, I know that with you all things are possible and I pray that you will help me achieve my goal of having a new girlfriend. In Jesus name I pray, Amen."

My Prayer: "Dear God, help me not make mistakes on my first dates with women. I want my first date to go smoothly and make a good impression on her so I can have a second date. In Jesus name I pray, Amen."

My Prayer: "Dear Jesus, make the plans for my love life and let nothing deter me from seeing them fulfilled. In Jesus name I pray, Amen."

My Prayer: "Dear God, help me overcome my shyness when I go to nightclubs. I get so nervous, fearful, and anxious when I think about approaching women that I am attracted to. Help me overcome these fears and give me the courage to approach women with a calm, cool, and confident attitude. In Jesus name I pray, Amen."

My Prayer: "Dear God, I pray that I don't make dumb dating mistakes and blunders that turn women off. In Jesus name I pray, Amen"

My Prayer: "Dear God, help me be a good driver when I'm on a date. I want to be a safe driver and not put my life, my date, and other people's lives in jeopardy. If I commit any of these driving sins help me overcome them. In Jesus name I pray, Amen."

Spiritual Comment and Prayer: These are the two most important prayers to say when you are dating:

1. When something good happens in your dating life say, "Thank you Jesus."
2. When things are going wrong in your dating life say, "Help me Lord."

My Prayer: "Dear Jesus, help me overcome feeling depressed and feeling sorry for myself when I don't have a woman to love in my life. Help me avoid having any pity parties. In Jesus name I pray, Amen."

My Prayer: "Dear God, please help me to be myself when dating and not try to pretend to be someone that I am not. In Jesus name I pray, Amen."

My Prayer: "Dear God, help me avoid being possessive, controlling, and smothering women that I date. I don't want to scare women off by being this way. In Jesus name I pray, Amen"

My Prayer: "Dear God, help me to get over and let go of my past relationships that did not work out. In Jesus name I pray, Amen"

My Prayer: "Lord please go ahead of me and prepare the way for me to succeed with women. Remove the obstacles to success that would cause me to fail with women. In Jesus name I pray, Amen"

My Prayer: "Dear God, please help me keep my ego in check and not depend on my looks to meet and attract women. Keep me from walking around with my nose up in the air thinking I'm God's gift to women. In Jesus name I pray, Amen."

My Prayer: "Dear God, I have a bad habit of using profanity around women and people in general. Please help me refrain from cursing when on a date, especially on a first date. Help me be a gentleman and treat women with respect. In Jesus name I pray, Amen."

My Prayer: "Jesus, fill me with your Holy Spirit and ease my restless mind in anticipation of going on my first date with the woman I'm so crazy about. In Jesus name I pray, Amen."

My Prayer: "Dear God, if I learn that a woman I am dating is unfaithful, make sure that I stop dating her and not give her a second chance. As the old saying goes "Once a cheater always a cheater." In Jesus name I pray, Amen."

My Prayer: "Dear God, please help me to stop smoking. Help me realize that this habit turns off a lot of women and can interfere with my dating women. More importantly, it can cause me some serious health problems. I want to live a long healthy life. In Jesus name I pray, Amen."

My Prayer: "Dear God, I have a bad habit of treating my date like one of the guys. Help me treat her with the utmost respect and like a lady. In Jesus name I pray, Amen."

My Prayer: "Dear God, I have a bad habit of thinking all women and people in general should think like I do. Help me realize that we are all unique individuals and all of us don't think alike. In Jesus name I pray, Amen."

My Prayer: "Jesus please help me to find good and kind words that will bring cheer to my date. In Jesus name I pray, Amen."

My Prayer: "Jesus, help me to remember that your power can lift me above any setback in my relationships with women. In Jesus name I pray, Amen."

My Prayer: "Dear God, I want to be a winner in the game of dating, love, and romance. Please help me follow the guidelines in this book to help me win with women. In Jesus name I pray, Amen."

My Prayer: "Dear God, don't let any of my fears of failure with women rear its ugly head in my mind. Keep my thoughts positive and focused on succeeding with women. In Jesus name I pray, Amen."

My Prayer: "Dear God, help me be sympathetic when I'm on a date. Help me refrain from offering solutions instead of being sympathetic and understanding with any problems she may discuss. In Jesus name I pray, Amen."

Spiritual Comment: When success comes my way with women I turn to you Jesus with a heart of thanksgiving.

My Prayer: "Dear God, help me realize that I am responsible for my happiness. Don't let me fall into the mental trap that I must be in a relationship to be happy. In Jesus name I pray, Amen"

My Prayer: "Dear God, help me develop a game plan for finding the right woman for me. Make sure I don't just settle for anyone just to be in a relationship. In Jesus name I pray, Amen."

My Prayer: "Dear God, help me have a positive and upbeat outlook when out on a date with women. Make sure I don't bitch, whine, and complain when I'm on a date because this will turn her off and make her not want to date me again. In Jesus name I pray, Amen."

My Prayer: "Dear God, I have a bad habit of putting things off when it comes to making an effort to meet, date, and attract women. Please help me get off of my dead ass and take action to meet, date, and attract women. Give me the attitude of, "Do it now" instead of procrastination. In Jesus name I pray, Amen."

My Prayer: "Dear God, I have a bad habit of taking control of all of the conversations on my dates. Help me give her equal time in talking and listen intently to what she has to say. In Jesus name I pray, Amen."

My Prayer: "Dear God, I have a bad habit of taking control of all of the conversations on my dates. Help me give her equal time in talking and listen intently to what she has to say. In Jesus name I pray, Amen."

My Prayer: "Dear God, help me to not talk about anything sexualwhen on a first date. She most likely will be offended and may not want to see me again. In Jesus name I pray, Amen."

My Prayer: "Dear God, help me take the time to get to know a woman before I fall in love with her. In Jesus name I pray, Amen."

My Prayer: "Dear Jesus, please help me improve my posture so I can make a better impression on women. Make sure that I stand straight with my shoulders back. I want to look like a West Point cadet...in Jesus name I pray...Amen"

My Prayer: "Dear God, help me overcome feeling depressed, lonely, and down in the dumps when I don't have a woman to date in my life, especially on the weekends. In Jesus name I pray, Amen."

My Prayer: "Dear Jesus, I ask you for a clear direction in my dating life. Guide my steps and show me the way. . In Jesus name I pray, Amen."

Spiritual Comment: I have never known a despondent day...It's because the joy of the Lord is the strength of my life.

My Prayer: "Dear God, help me overcome my fears in approaching women that are holding me back from meeting women. In Jesus name I pray, Amen."

My Prayer: "Dear God, please help me from getting involved with women that are no good for me. Protect me from these women who would not be good for me. In Jesus name I pray, Amen"

Spiritual Comment: There is nothing in my life that does not come from you, Jesus. This includes that special lady you will send me that seems heaven sent.

My Prayer: "Dear God, help me get over and bury all my negative experiences in dating. I want to forget them and focus on having positive experiences in dating for my future. In Jesus name I pray, Amen."

My Prayer: "Thank you Jesus for the unbreakable promise that you hear and answer my prayers for somebody to love. In Jesus name I pray, Amen."

About the Author Don Diebel

I'd like to introduce myself: I'm Don Diebel (America's #1 Singles Expert) and one of the nation's leading experts on dating and relationships, guest speaker on several TV and radio shows, featured in print interviews, dating consultant, and I have helped thousands of men win at the game of love with my phenomenal best-selling books, dating articles, and dating advice at: www.getgirls.com

Also, I am President and owner of Gemini Publishing Company and getgirls.com, which specializes in Books, eBooks, Audio Cassettes, Videos, CDs, DVDs, and Pheromone Products to help you successfully meet, date, attract, and seduce women located at: https://www.getgirls.com

Affiliation: Doctorate of Publishing - Presented by Para Publishing - November 6, 1988.

Graduate of the Key West College of Millionaires - October 11, 1990.

I am the author of the following best-selling books:

The Complete Guide to Meeting Women...Featured in the Playboy Catalog and on the Jimmy Fallon Tonight Show

200 Guaranteed and Proven Ways to Meet, Date, Attract, and Seduce Women

How to Pick Up Women in Nightclubs

1001 Best Pick Up Lines...Sure-Fire Opening Lines for Meeting, Dating, Attracting, and Seducing Women

200 Guaranteed Ways to Succeed with Women...Everything You Need to Know on How to Meet, Date, and Attract Women

The Houston Entertainment and Dating Guide

How to Pick Up Women in Discos

How to Improve Your Golf with S/A Hypnotism

Finding Mr. Right

The Complete Guide to Meeting Men and Finding Mr. Right

100 Places to Take a Date

Dating with Jesus...A Daily Spiritual Guide for Men On How to Meet, Date, and Attract Women

How to Use the Power of Jesus to Help You Meet, Date, and Attract Women

Help me Jesus: 365 Daily Spiritual Devotions to Help Men Meet, Date, and Attract Women

How to Use the Power of Jesus to Help You Meet, Date, and Attract Men

Help me Lord: 365 Daily Spiritual Devotions to Help Women Meet, Date, and Attract Men

Follow me on Facebook at: www.facebook.com/singlesexpert

Follow me on my How to Meet, Date, and Attract Women Blog at: www.dondiebel.blogspot.com

Follow me on Twitter (X) at: www.twitter.com/singlesexperts

Follow me on Instagram at:_www.instagram.com/singlesexpert/

Follow me on Pinterest at: www.pinterest.com/dondiebel

www.ingramcontent.com/pod-product-compliance
Lightning Source LLC
Chambersburg PA
CBHW030105070426
42448CB00037B/981